The Supernatural YOU

Brenda Kunneman

HOUSE
A STRANG COMPANY

The Supernatural You by Brenda Kunneman
Published by Charisma House
A Strang Company
600 Rinehart Road
Lake Mary, Florida 32746
www.strangbookgroup.com

Design Director: Bill Johnson
Cover design by Amanda Potter

Library of Congress Cataloging-in-Publication Data

Kunneman, Brenda.
  The supernatural you / by Brenda Kunneman. -- 1st ed.
    p. cm.
  ISBN 978-1-59979-780-9
 1. Holy Spirit. 2. Christian life. I. Title.

  BT123.K86 2009
  248.4--dc22

                          2009018915

10 11 12 13 14 — 10 9 8 7 6 5
Printed in the United States of America

This book is dedicated to the Holy Spirit, whose power and anointing have transformed lives around the world and set the church on fire.

CONTENTS

Chapter One

THE SUPERNATURAL GOD
IS IN YOU

W HAT A MESS!" we both kept saying again and
again as we threw our hands in the air. My
husband and I had spent the entire day going
through old boxes of things we had collected over the years.
We had set aside several days to clean out closets and storage
spaces. We found countless things we forgot we owned. Do
you have some boxes like that—the ones where you sort of
know what is in them, but then again, not really? Most of us
have scores of them.

In those boxes we found old magazines, yearbooks, old
cassette tapes, pictures, and keepsakes. Many had developed
a musty smell that comes from years of storage. Then we
came to the boxes of things we had saved from our early years
together of marriage and ministry. After hours of sorting,
I found it. It was a piece of paper from a time in our lives
when it seemed that our dreams for the future were crum-
bling one by one. It was a prayer list we had made, much of
which seemed so far-fetched. Some of the items on the list
were immediate needs that existed at the time, while others
were larger dreams and things we were asking God to do in
the years to come, much of which would take an absolute
miracle to accomplish.

The day we wrote it out years before, we had hung that long list of seemingly impossible requests on our refrigerator. Every day we walked by it, and we would place our hands on it and pray. We spoke aloud each time, reminding the Lord we were expecting miracles. We quoted the Scripture verses we were trusting in regard to it. We declared that each item would come to pass and we would see the hand of God move. We spoke over the list believing for God's intervention, even when it felt like we weren't seeing it.

Shortly thereafter, we moved to a different house and, along with the rest of our household items, packed up that list of prayer requests. Well, you know how it goes. You don't always unpack all those boxes. Actually, a few moves later and nearly two decades of marriage later, the number of unpacked boxes in the garage and basement grew.

Then finally on clean-out day, I read that list again written almost twenty years ago. My eyes filled with tears as I read it. I suddenly realized that God had not only answered the seemingly small things, but over the years He had also answered *every* item on the list, way beyond even what we wrote down. He even answered the things that seemed impossible. Again, in a flash, I was reminded of all the miracles that we had seen during the last several years. We had seen the power of God revealed from heaven again and again. The things we had seen God do were nothing short of miraculous, and it was mostly all related to what was on that list!

At that moment, we were not only reminded of God's enduring faithfulness (and we apologized to the Lord for not acknowledging His answers to these prayers sooner), but we also realized something else. It was that every time we were putting our hand on that list taped to the fridge we were releasing the power of God to work on our behalf.

The supernatural God inside us was releasing miracles; a river was flowing and bringing the answer, and it didn't stop flowing until every request was answered, even though we didn't realize it was happening at the time.

I have learned from this experience not just that God lives in us, but that the *supernatural* God lives in us. He wants His supernatural power to flow through us to accomplish the miraculous and do the impossible in our circumstances.

I was talking with a woman one afternoon who I knew was struggling through a series of trials in her life—serious trials. Of course, she was a Christian, but her outlook for her future felt hopeless. Her take on the whole situation was that she was powerless to do anything but wait and see what God would do. Sure, I knew she was committed to trust God, even if the outcome wasn't what she hoped. However, let's face it; she wanted the same outcome we all want—the same outcome we wanted when we made our prayer list. She wanted her trial to result in a miracle. She wanted a supernatural intervention of God to turn her situation around for the better.

If we are honest with ourselves, that is really what we all want when we come to God, isn't it? We say that we are content to walk out the trial in God's peace until hopefully it passes, and even if it doesn't, we will be content that God has it all under control. But deep down, what we really want is for the supernatural power of God to come in, just like in the days of the Bible, to overcome and ultimately eradicate the trial we are facing. We want healing where there was disease. We want financial stability where there once was upheaval. We want strength in the place of weakness. We want the power of God to rescue us from the pain of today so we can rise up a new person tomorrow. Maybe what we have yet to realize is that the power of God is already there. It's in you in the person of the Holy Spirit, ready to work and ready to move and flow. Acts 1:8 says, "But ye shall receive power, after that the Holy Ghost is come upon you: and ye shall be witnesses unto me both in Jerusalem, and in all Judaea, and in Samaria, and unto the uttermost part of the earth."

Now the word *power* here literally means "explosive power." If you were to make a comparison to it, you would probably think of dynamite. It is the supernatural power of God's Spirit being downloaded into your own spirit. When the fullness of God's Spirit is in you, there is power, and it is the same power that performed the miracle of raising Jesus Christ from the dead (Rom. 8:11).

THE SUPERNATURAL RIVER OF GOD

Jesus referred to the source of God's supernatural power like a river. This is one of the most powerful principles in the Bible. One of the most prominent scriptures about this is in John 7:37–39. If you really delve into these particular verses woven through Scripture, your walk with the Lord will be revolutionized.

> If any man thirst, let him come unto me, and drink. He that believeth on me, as the scripture hath said, out of his belly shall flow rivers of living water. (But this spake he of the Spirit, which they that believe on him should receive: for the Holy Ghost was not yet given; because that Jesus was not yet glorified.)

Jesus begins by saying that when you are thirsty, you should come to Him for a drink. Why? Because He is the river of God's glory, and all spiritual resources from heaven flow in the current of that river. Everything we need to relieve our "thirst" is in there. There is healing in there, deliverance in there, relief, finances, right relationships, creative miracles, peace, joy, and restoration. Whatever our need might be is flowing in that river.

Think of the areas in your life that are currently in a drought or places where you have needs. These are the places that seem to have no solutions. Things are dry and desperately need some answers. Jesus gave a direct solution to relieve that thirst. It was, "Come unto me, and drink." Now, for many of us that statement is nothing more than poetic rhetoric that we aren't sure exactly how we should respond to. So we fall back on the pillow and reflect on how peaceful the statement makes us feel and assume that is taking a drink. But we don't actually *do* anything! We think drinking from the fountain of Jesus is taking a deep breath and thinking calmly about Him until the pressure from our problem seems to melt away. When we get up and nothing has changed, it feels more fruitful to just turn on the television and get advice from the psychologist's program. We think perhaps that will get us on the road to repair as we try our best to keep Jesus in view!

Is that scene familiar to you? Anyone can certainly get advice from the doctor's television show to help, but good advice doesn't necessarily provide you any supernatural power. It may give you "head" power, but without the force of spiritual power fueling you first, called the anointing, you will find yourself unfulfilled and only guessing if you are doing the right thing. You will be left to depend on natural wisdom alone, which is deeply limited.

When we are dry and thirsty, the lasting solution does not begin with quick advice and actions; it begins with a flow of spiritual power, a flow from the river of the Spirit. Jesus said that *He* was that river of power. This is where so many of us miss it. We work something out naturally first and later try to add God to it; then we reason why our course of action was His plan all along or we question God as to why we failed.

It is like trying to clean the dirt from the carpet without first plugging in the vacuum. It is impossible to do without the power first. The vacuum cleaner might be the best method, you may even have the best model they make, but without power the best answer will become a pointless effort. I have tried many times to make spiritual decisions this way—eeny, meeny, miny, moe! Then I look at all the pros and cons and see if they line up. There is no power in it.

You look at what seems biblical and hope you made the right decision. Thinking through your decisions this way is good, just like choosing the right vacuum, but the missing link is what Jesus said—"Come unto me, and drink." He was saying, "I am the river and anointing of God. I have the power you need that will *cause* the right thing to happen." It is like an injection of vitamins! We have to connect with the river of power, just as you plug the vacuum into the wall. Jesus was presenting Himself as the power source, a river of water that you fill up with before you attempt anything else.

THE RIVER WITHIN YOU

We can know without any doubt that Jesus *is* the water source we need, but it does us no good if we don't have a map to locate the fountain. We have to know how to take the drink. For the river of God to be your resource in life, you have to know where to find it. *It is not just thinking about Jesus and trying to feel victorious.* You have to find where He is flowing from and tap into that flow.

As we saw in John 7:38, Jesus said, "He that believeth on

me, as the scripture hath said, out of his belly shall flow rivers of living water." In other words, "Whoever believes that I am dependable water to drink from shall find the supernatural river coming out of *his own* belly." Your own belly is your spirit. It shall come out of YOU in the form of living water. Now, living water is not just any water. It is "powerized" water. If water has an electric current running through it, you can definitely say that it is living. When you dip your finger in it, believe me, you will know its power. The river Jesus was talking about was the unlimited power of God. Where do you find its flow? According to John 7:39, it is found flowing from the Holy Spirit who lives in *your* spirit.

In the Bible, references to rivers and water flowing *from* God repeatedly show the source of them coming from inside of us. This has always been God's intention, to work in you and through you. Like many people, I always pictured it differently. I had always envisioned some river actually flowing out of heaven and landing on my head to refresh me with God's presence. I pictured the rain of God landing on me like physical rain. Do you ever see it like that?

Years ago in many church circles, we used to recite an old saying that said, "Get under the spout where the glory comes out!" Today we sing phrases like "rain on me" or "glory fall on us" and the like. Now what we are trying to say is that we all need to get to where God is moving so we can experience the tangible presence of His Spirit and feel Him in a physical way. There is not necessarily anything wrong with that, but I believe the reason we find God moving in certain places more than others is that the people gathered have found how to tap into the river of the Holy Spirit within them.

The key to activate the supernatural river flow of the Holy Spirit is to look within us because that is where He lives.

Know that His power is already present. We just have to know how to unleash it so we can live from it regardless of where we are or what we feel at that moment.

The best way to get consistent and dependable fulfillment and results in your life is to learn how to drink from the river of the Spirit in you. We cannot only depend on the prayer line, deliverance room, church altar, counseling center, or receiving a personal prophecy to get our answers, because these things may not always be available. Instead, they come to support the anointing that is flowing from within. But if we don't know how to depend on that flow within, we will live from struggle to struggle all our lives.

Zechariah 14:8 says, "And it shall be in that day, that living waters shall go out from Jerusalem; half of them toward the former sea, and half of them toward the hinder sea: in summer and in winter shall it be." Here we see the same living waters we have been talking about issuing from Jerusalem. We know from Revelation 21:2 and Jeremiah 33:16 that we, the body of Christ, are the picture of the spiritual Jerusalem. This verse in Zechariah paints a prophetic picture of these living waters proceeding from us. They proceed from the church corporately, and they flow out of us individually. Here it says that the flow of the river is not affected by the season. That means it will work and flow regardless of atmosphere or temperature. It is an ever-present river of supernatural power that will work in adverse circumstances.

When you need something from God, you can begin to look to Him inside of your own spirit. That is where His power is residing. That is what Jesus said: "out of your spirit." That is the first key in getting the power of God to work in your life: receiving the filling of the Holy Spirit and looking down inside *you* to find the anointing of God ready to flow over your situation.

WHERE THE SUPERNATURAL RIVER BEGINS

I came from the typical Christian family, at least for the most part. We believed in salvation through the cross, went to church at least half of the year, and tried to live decent lives. Truthfully, my parents really loved the Lord in the way they knew, and our family was close. My father was in the military, so we moved around a lot. That also meant we changed churches a lot, so there was no real accountability or commitment, which is a convenience for many nominal Christians. If life was unhappy in one town, you could always count on the fact that a move was on the way. Occasionally, my parents attended available Bible studies with other, mostly military, families. It was the picture of the average American Christian.

In the military base chapels, which we sometimes attended, there were always people from all sorts of spiritual backgrounds. They were mostly denominational, but there was always the one, yes, that one Pentecostal believing person who invaded every military assignment we had. It seemed that no matter how hard we tried to avoid them, they were always there. My parents were not really against it, but they were just not for it either. One day I asked my mom about it. She replied with a simple, "It is something that some people believe in, but we don't do that." "OK, so I guess we don't," I thought.

When I was a teenager, our family experienced some minor family troubles. You know, the kind where the entire family lives on the fence between Christianity and a secular lifestyle and the secular half is dominating the two. Outside of a radical and powerful Christian life, a person does not have the ability to deal correctly with all the problems life presents. Eventually you will lose your way somewhere. In that light, we needed a change. We were void of any real Christian power. I had one particular teenage confrontation with my dad, and one by one, we finally concluded that our family needed a God intervention. We didn't know it at the time, but God was at work and arranging something that would turn us around forever.

My dad had a Christian co-worker with whom he had been talking about the Bible. He went to a charismatic church, of course. He and my dad worked in a small room together, so there was just no avoiding it. There was work and talk. However, he was really committed to God, much more than we had been. He talked about things we hadn't heard, like the miracle power of God. He talked about the Holy Spirit as if He actually did powerful things. He also shared stories of modern-day people getting healed by God's power and so on. He and his family talked about the power of God in a way that we were unfamiliar with even as Christians. They talked about angels working in their lives, casting out demons, and sensing the anointing. They were ignited somehow. When they talked about God this way, I actually began to feel something physically. My stomach would jump up and down with excitement because for the first time I felt a touch from God in a way that felt like electricity. We didn't know it then, but we were craving an experience with the tangible power of God, because our previous Christianity was so lifeless. It was obvious by the fruit of our lives.

We learned about the Holy Spirit of the Book of Acts and learned that according to Acts 2:38–39 we could have that same experience. I got ahold of a little book about the baptism of the Holy Spirit, and one night before bed, I read it, trying to understand every word! *"Hmmm,"* I thought to myself, "I want that!"

For days, all I could think about was the Holy Spirit and this powerful feeling that I had begun to taste, or feel. I read every book I could get my hands on about the Holy Spirit because for the first time, I had felt Him. I wanted to be filled with the Spirit the way I saw all through the Book of Acts, because they had power. Up to this point in my Christian experience, I didn't have much of any; these people, however, had power to raise up a cripple man, rebuke evil spirits, and overcome their problems. "That's it," I thought. "I am going to receive the Holy Spirit."

So I determined to ask God for the supernatural person of the Holy Spirit to fill me to overflowing just like the Book of Acts. I figured the best place to have that kind of supernatural experience was in the family bathroom, because I figured no one would bother me there! I remembered a book I had read that said, "When you ask the Holy Spirit to fill you, you may begin to hear some words or sounds down inside of you, so just speak them out and don't worry about what they sound like." (See Acts 2:3–4.) Even though I was alone, I was still kind of embarrassed to try it. I guess I thought someone might hear through the door! Actually, I was afraid to hear it myself.

Throwing caution to the wind, I closed my eyes tightly and started mumbling under my breath. One syllable was all that came out for about two minutes. "Well," I thought, "that's all I hear down inside me, so this must be it—I guess." It was actually quite ordinary rather than feeling supernatural. With that, I left the bathroom.

I guess I had expected at least to see a vision or something.

I mean, where were the lightning bolts and stuff like that? I thought I was supposed to feel a wind, like the Book of Acts; you know, with some real signs and wonders.

I wasn't too sure if I had really experienced anything, but somehow as days went by, I couldn't get past it, so I decided to just keep saying those syllables to myself to see if I felt anything. I figured that is what I had to do to get something to happen. Sometimes I had a few new syllables, a little more here and a little more there. I asked myself again, "This has to be it, right? Lord, do I have the Holy Spirit or not?" I heard nothing.

Finally, one day I can only remember that I determined within myself that this was going to be it regardless. In my mind, I had the Holy Spirit whether I really did or not! All I knew was that I wanted to keep experiencing the super-natural God of the Bible I had begun to feel for the first time. So, I just started telling everyone I was baptized in the Spirit and just never went back to believing otherwise. Now, that's how I was filled with the Holy Ghost. There was no pomp and circumstance; there was just asking God for it, a few syllables, and deciding that was it.

Yet something started changing in the months to follow. Suddenly being a Christian was a daily and exciting priority, unlike the boredom of it before. I noticed that the Bible wasn't boring anymore either. Here I was a teenager, and suddenly I detested the sound of secular music. On my own, I threw away my entire collection of rock music. I couldn't get enough of God. Something was different. I would liter-ally feel God on me, so to speak. Something had happened to me that I loved, even though I didn't understand it all then. Yes, something was definitely deposited inside of me. What I didn't realize yet was that there was something more in there than just a good feeling about God. This was to be the beginning of where the river of God's power was going to flow through my entire life and cause supernatural things to happen.

WHERE DID THE POWER GO?

When I was first filled with the Holy Spirit, I was still in high school. I didn't know yet that He wanted to flow from me like a river everywhere I went so my needs could be met in any circumstance. I went to a denominational Christian school, and nobody seemed to understand the exciting things I was experiencing. The way that I knew and loved the Holy Spirit was not going to be accepted by them. They even found it offensive. It was easy to become discouraged.

We lived in a small town, and churches were few. We went to a newly formed, tiny Spirit-filled church that met in an old feed store. It didn't have much going, but it was all we had. We went regularly, but it became apparent right away that I would have to get and maintain some of my spiritual needs on my own.

I spent my time in my room, reading the Bible and praying in the Spirit. I listened to preaching tapes until I could almost recite them. As I did this, I began to notice something happening. The things I needed from God came, and my prayers started getting answered in supernatural ways! I started to experience miracles and incredible moments with the living God. Amazingly, I began to see my future in the ministry. I would have dreams and pictures come to me. They were so clear. It was as if I was living in it right then. They were so real, and as a result, I started to practice preaching in my teen bedroom with an ironing board as my pulpit.

Then afterward, I would go to school, into an atmosphere

of resistance, and feel the need to hide everything. If I tried even once to mention any of it, I was met with determined opposition. I was pressured to suppress the power of God, and every time I would hide it. Then I would have to go home and try to refuel and start over. It seemed like a never-ending season of spiritual stalemate—no real failure, but no powerful growth either. I wasn't trying to compromise; I was just trying to survive unnecessary controversy. The problem was I had trouble keeping the power flowing under those circumstances because I would get discouraged. I could only seem to keep it going under the right circumstances. I felt so defeated. It was hard to stay strong when there was no outside support.

This is where the rubber meets the road when it comes to the power of God in your life. Of all the things I have heard in my years as a Christian, the one I hear most often is, "When I am in a trial, I just don't know where the power goes. I find myself struggling! I want to be strong, but…" Many people seem to struggle with staying strong in the Spirit when they are under the pressure to fail, compromise, and sin. Some just give up standing. That is just how the devil works, and it is how he easily defeats many believers.

DELIVERED FROM RESTRICTED-RIVER SYNDROME

I like to think of this type of struggle as "restricted-river syndrome," and many Christians suffer from it. The symptoms are like this: you get all filled up with the anointing of God and feel like you are ready to take on the world and stomp out the devil at the same time. The Spirit of God feels so strong inside you. But when the right atmosphere is gone and replaced with opposition, your river flow is cut off and you cannot seem to maintain enough supply to keep you on top.

Many believers just accept the idea that they simply cannot expect God to come in with a supernatural miracle. Some even go as far as forgetting about that power source altogether. Then they look for answers elsewhere instead of depending on the anointing inside of them. The power seems like it is nowhere around because their emotions are over-whelmed under the weight of the problem.

When you cannot keep the supernatural flow of God going inside you when you face a problem or meet with resistance, you may be dealing with restricted-river syndrome. The anointing in you tends to feel like a trickle in comparison to the trials and responsibilities of life. You keep going to church to get pumped again, but the supply barely carries you until Monday afternoon. Then after you get home from work, the excitement of Sunday seems miles away. It is like filling a bucket with a hole in the bottom.

This is why people go from conference to conference, and even to church every week, and never seem to enjoy a lasting change in their life. They keep doing what it takes to keep that freshness they received from the Holy Spirit, but they struggle to keep the flow lasting long enough to really affect something. It becomes a repeated cycle of short-circuiting the power of God. I know many people who have wonderful "church" moments but can't survive their workweek. The power they were flooded with is cut off, and they are back to seeking the next "God experience" for some refreshing.

Of course we need to keep doing what it takes to get refreshed, but what good is it if our refreshing doesn't make us stronger than the attacks of the devil? We need the power of the Holy Spirit to be powerful enough to deal with the daily things we face in our lives.

Are you familiar with restricted-river syndrome? I was! This is just what was happening to me. Determined I could not live on this roller coaster for long, I prayed to the Lord. The folks at my school were finding every way to unravel what I believed, even though I tried hard not to provoke them. Then God began to open my eyes to something. The Holy Spirit brought a verse of Scripture to light, even though I had read it before. It was so simple, but it was the very thing I was missing. It is the beginning revelation we need if we want to manifest the power of God, even when we are being tempted or resisted.

Look at Proverbs 4:23. It says, "Keep thy heart with all diligence; for out of it are the issues of life." First of all, this verse says that there are *issues* of life. What that means is that there are *forces* that cause life to spring forth. It is like the carbon bubbles inside a soda. Those forces cause the soda to "come alive," and when you taste it, you know it is there. It is the same way with the Holy Spirit. God, in the person of Holy Spirit, is the "issue" or "force" that is producing life in everything He touches. But here is the first key to getting that life to touch your situation. Notice where it says the life comes from. The forceful, life-producing currents come from within you. The verse says that they come from your heart, or from your spirit. The Holy Spirit inside you is pushing or forcing His life to flow out of you, and it never leaves you. Keeping the flow of God's power working all the time begins when we realize that it is not flowing from out there somewhere in space. *It is going to flow from within you.* Even in cases where someone else comes along to minister something to you, it still requires the supernatural inside you to connect with it for you to experience results.

I didn't realize, when I was at school, that the Holy Spirit within me had a river of supply available everywhere I went. I was going to school every day feeling all alone. It was as if I would enter that atmosphere, and *poof*, that supernatural presence was gone. This is just what the devil wants. He wants you to feel isolated and alone so you forget there is a supernatural river within you. He wants to keep you feeling deserted from God's power. Satan knows that if he can keep you only focused on your last church or prayer experience and how far away it feels, then you will feel hopeless. He wants you to forget completely about the supply inside you *right now*. No, not just inside the TV preacher but inside *you*.

I realized that I had to go back to the same attitude that I had in the bathroom that day when I received the Holy Spirit. I had decided that day that no matter what, *this is it right here and now.* The power of God is in me. You have to determine that you have the ability to operate in the supernatural power of God in every circumstance. It doesn't mean you have to do or even say anything right then and there. Sometimes if you are around people, you may not be able to. You just need to know that the power of God is on you and that it is working regardless of what it feels like. If you don't stay conscious of this fact, restricted-river syndrome will set in, and you will not feel like the kind of believer who can overcome any bondage, problem, disease, or trial that comes your way. It will cause the power of God to be hindered.

The very reason many people are not overcoming their problems is because they are convinced in the back of their minds that they are powerless! They have far more confidence in the conference speaker's power than their own. They want to hear another prophecy in order to be convinced that God is still with them and at work in their situation.

This is also what happened to the disciples in Matthew 17:14–21 when they had tried to cast a demon out of a young boy but couldn't do it. They had the power to do it because Jesus had given it to them in Matthew 10:1, but on this occasion it wasn't working. They asked Jesus why they couldn't cast the demon out, and He gave them the reason in verse 20: "Because of your unbelief." Even though they had the power to do it, they didn't believe it. Jesus had already given them everything they needed for it, but their inability to believe that they had it stopped a miracle. It stopped their supernatural flow.

Doesn't this sound like many in the body of Christ today? We can't see ourselves carrying that level of power within us. I was filled with the Holy Spirit that day because I was confident that I personally could tap into His power all by myself, and I wasn't thrown off by how it felt in the beginning. When I realized I could keep going back to that same source of power and that it was always working through me, I began to walk in a new level of the supernatural and of breakthrough.

In fact, the same thing was taking place all those years ago when, in spite of the challenges at hand, we kept putting our hands on the prayer list that hung on the fridge. Sometimes it felt like nothing was happening, but it was! God's Spirit was working through us every time we put our hands on that list and prayed in the Spirit.

So many people don't realize the river of God inside is waiting to be pushed like the blinking icon at the bottom menu of your computer that says, "Install Updates Now." It is already in you according to Proverbs 4:23, but we are often busy looking to everything else to find it. That river of power doesn't have to manifest only at the conference, church, or prayer line. It is already in your spirit trying to flood its way out to help you! How often have we been in a difficult situation and forgotten about the power of the anointing in us just pressing to be released?

Some years later after high school, I took a job at a bank. I had worked there for some time, and the time came for my first performance review. By this time, I knew much more about how to resist the restricted-river syndrome. I made a habit now of praying in the Spirit and keeping God's Word in my mouth. I often wrote scriptures on index cards and brought them to work with me. I kept them in my purse, and every so often during break opportunities I would read them and recite them under my breath, reminding myself that God was working through His Spirit in me. I needed that in a worldly environment.

My boss, who was not a Christian as far as I knew, called me into the conference room where my review was to be held. She asked me to sit down across the table from her. When she sat down, she made one short comment about my job and, then to my surprise, changed the subject to talk about a serious disease that was in her body. Moments later, she began to cry and shake uncontrollably. Then she said, "I feel something. I feel God! Please pray for me!" I tell you it was a good thing the curtains were closed! Although I was initially shocked, I jumped on the opportunity. I put my hand on her and prayed, and the miracle power of God came and healed her.

Now how did she know I had anything to help her? I didn't even make a conscious effort to witness to her. I believe it was because this time, much different from my high school experience, I entered the place with the river of God flowing from my spirit. What can happen when we realize what lies inside us and we let that power flow from us? We will step into the supernatural things of God everywhere we go, even in situations where we least expect it.

CHARACTERISTICS OF THE RIVER OF GOD

When you think about natural rivers, you can see why the Bible compares the power of God and His anointing to them. Rivers have unique characteristics from other bodies of water that emulate the anointing of the Holy Spirit. The way they function is very much the way the river of your spirit is supposed to work. Here are four characteristics about rivers that correlate to the river of our spirit. It will help us understand how this river of God inside us operates.

1. Rivers are made of water.

Water is one of the most powerful substances on the earth, making up two-thirds of the entire planet. We read in Genesis 1:2 that before anything was created, the Spirit of God moved upon the face of the waters. Where did He move? Over the surface of the earth's waters. Several other translations indicate that His Spirit was actually stirring the waters, creating waves or a current. He caused the water to have movement. This was the first example of the *move* of the Holy Spirit, and it is no coincidence that His moving had to do with the water. The Spirit of the Lord was moving through water from the very first verse in the Bible. There is something very powerful and prophetic about water because His Spirit is represented in the movement and flow of it.

Notice that in many eastern religions, the worshipers

always try to conjure evil spirits over water through certain water rituals. It is very interesting how many demonic activities and movements on the earth are found around water, whether it be in bodies of water or in storms. I believe Satan knows that the power of God's Spirit correlates to water, and his desire is to create a counterfeit appearance. He wants to make the world believe that he is in control against the Spirit of God by using water, the most powerful force on the earth.

Water is also a cleansing substance. It has the ability to purify like nothing else. Rivers actually have a built-in filtering system. The movement of the water adds oxygen and promotes cleaning. The movement and operation of God's Spirit inside you flows and moves to promote life and purity.

Several years ago I was in prayer, and I asked the Lord to purify every area of my life. It is important to pray along those lines on a regular basis. It keeps your heart clean. During the prayer, I physically recall smelling an odor that entered the room, which resembled the smell of some kind of cleaner or bleach-like soap. I could literally feel soap and water in my spirit, and I could smell it! No one in the house was using cleaners or doing the laundry. I remember sensing such a feeling of purity and cleanliness. I was aware of the aroma for some time after that. It was a supernatural experience from the river of God in my spirit. It was wonderful! Malachi 3:2 says, "For he is like a refiner's fire, and like fullers' soap." The Holy Spirit within you works like spiritual soap and water. It will give you a daily spiritual shower.

2. Rivers have a strong current.

Rivers are also unique in that they are the one body of water with a current moving in one firm direction. When they become full at the floodwater stage, nothing can stop them! If you have ever seen a river overflow its banks, you know very quickly that nothing can stand in its way. Raging water can remove large buildings, bridges, trucks, and even some trees. The result of a raging flood is devastating. It is easy to see why Jesus referred to His Spirit inside of us like a river! When the floodwaters of God come from within you, they are designed to wash over every obstacle of resistance. In other words, the devil cannot create a barrier big enough to stand up to it. Know that whatever wall seems to be standing against you right now is vulnerable to the floodwaters coming from your spirit. It is the Holy Ghost within you pouring out against it to cause a breakthrough for you.

3. Rivers always have tributaries.

Main rivers always have smaller rivers or little creeks that branch off them. These are called tributaries. These tributaries provide up close and personal help to the environment and communities that the main river does not reach. They give easier access to people or animals, and they provide water to particular locations. They are like a powerful extension of the main river designed to provide for a specific area. The Holy Spirit preplans everything, doesn't He? It is no wonder that in John 7:38 Jesus said, "Out of [your] belly shall flow *rivers...*"—plural. It is not just one river, but there are many rivers coming from your spirit, each designed to uniquely minister to every issue you face. The Spirit of God has a flow that applies to everything you could possibly need. There are enough rivers flowing from your spirit to influence every situation with a special anointing tailor-made just for that area.

A little over a year ago, my husband and I were both having some trouble sleeping at night. Either we tossed and turned, or I, particularly, would wake up with kinks and pains. We couldn't figure out the reason, so I began to pull from the Spirit of God within me by praying in the Spirit. Good sleep is pretty important! One night I had a dream, and I saw myself in a store purchasing new pillows for the bed. In the dream, I "felt" myself sleeping on them. The dream was so real that when I woke up in the morning, I couldn't dismiss it, and I went to a discount store to find some pillows. I told my husband that I needed to spend some good money on pillows because they were prophetic ones! He just looked at me, but I was on a mission. I prayed on the way and asked the Spirit of God in me to lead me to the perfect ones. I knew for sure that the Holy Spirit was telling me that our pillows were the problem. The Holy Spirit will provide the supernatural power even for something as simple as your pillow!

At the store I looked over every one they had and finally chose one, but they only had one of them. Very disappointed, I went to the next store, and the exact same thing happened. Getting a little frustrated, I went to one last store trying to obey my dream. Every pillow I had chosen up to this point didn't have a match. Some of them were even a little pricey too. I finally went to an outlet and found some designer pillows that sold for less than half the price, and there were oodles of them! While I purchased them, the clerk mentioned to me that she had bought some pillows recently, naming the ones I had tried to buy at the other stores. I didn't tell her that I had looked at those, but then she said they were terrible pillows and hoped the ones I was buying here were better! Thank God, those other pillows were all out of stock! I got the new pillows, and they were incredible. We have rested perfectly every night. When the rivers of my spirit started flowing, I had enough confidence in the power within me to stir it up by praying in the Spirit. Through God's Spirit, I had exactly what I needed to address the problem.

The rivers of your spirit can address even the smallest of issues. You possess a different river, or anointing, for every thing you need. Out of your belly shall flow *rivers* of living water from the Spirit of God!

4. River waters can recede.

River waters are most unique in how they fill up and recede. Oceans don't do that. Lakes can fill up, but you never hear about large lakes flooding things the same way rivers always do. Rivers fill up and become unpredictable. Rivers can also dry up. This cycle of filling and receding can happen repeatedly in a short period of time. God compared His Spirit in you to a river because He knew that the full flow of that anointing could be strong at times but then recede. It is not because God designed it to recede; it is because He wanted you to be aware that you have to keep yourself full of that living water. If not, you begin to lose the power of it. You become dry and thirsty. You have to fill the well so you can drink the water of it again.

Luke 11:24 says, "When the unclean spirit is gone out of a man, he walketh through dry places..." We also find in Luke 8:26 that the man possessed by a legion of demons was driven into the wilderness by these evil spirits. When Jesus was tempted by the devil in Luke 4:1, the confrontation was also in the wilderness. Demons seem to have an attraction to dead, dry things, don't they? Now Satan tries to gain *control* of the earth's water, but he loves to make his *home* around the dry, lifeless things. Demons want to hang around where there is no flow, no anointing, and where the waters of the Spirit have receded. That is why they love dead religion; there is no life in it, and the preaching is so dry you can almost see dust flying through the air.

To resist demons hanging around, you can fill your well so full that it will spill over its banks and bring fear to every evil spirit. This is God's intention. Have you ever been in a serious storm and seen the banks of a river get right up to the bridge you were crossing? It can be terrifying and very intimidating. This is how demons feel when the banks of your river begin to rise. They probably begin to say, "Hold on, boys! I think we are in danger of a flood. We had better get out of here." They are afraid of the supernatural rivers of your spirit.

Once you become fully aware that the Holy Spirit in you has deposited a supernatural river of power available at every moment, your Christianity will never be the same. You can learn to tap into it whenever you need it.

Too many believers have lived paycheck-to-paycheck style, going from one experience with God to another and trying hard to hold on in between. They wait until the next prophecy, which can't come too soon. They look for every reason to get in the prayer line, even when the preacher doesn't call out their particular need. They desperately pray for an open vision and even try harder not to keep committing the same sins. But they forget about the power within them that the Holy Spirit has provided to deal with these issues. They never learn that the supernatural power of the Holy Spirit in them is a river, and they do not know how to depend on that resource of power. It is like having one million dollars in the bank but only drawing out one dollar per week to survive on.

This power within was the river Jesus was talking about. It was the river of God deposited in every Spirit-filled believer designed to handle the opposing pressures of life, not just to make you feel better but to actually deal with it. The source of God is not coming from out there somewhere; it is coming from within you, and it stays with you everywhere you go.

Maintaining it begins with changing our thinking from seeing the anointing as some outward experience to seeing it coming from within instead. The flow of the Spirit wakes up with you. It gets in the car with you and goes to work with you. It is ready to address whatever faces you and is there to deliver you, speak to you, and help you. It doesn't leave, because it is a part of you. It will heal you, and it will help you overcome sin and live holy. It will help you know God intimately so that your mind takes on a new outlook.

I didn't know it back when I was a teenager, but this Holy Spirit brought with Him a supernatural flow of power that was going to ignite my walk with God. It was a river that I didn't know existed. It was a supernatural well inside my very own spirit. It was working when we put our hands on those prayer requests hanging on the fridge all those years ago, and it worked that day in my job review. You too must be convinced today that if God's Spirit is in you, the resource is also in you to accomplish whatever you need. Yes, the supernatural river of God is inside *you*.

Chapter Two

THE PIVOTAL EVENT THAT
CHANGED HISTORY

T HERE HE WAS, standing before the Lord crying, "Lord, please show me Your glory!" These were the words of Moses in Exodus 33:18 as he spoke with the Lord in a face-to-face encounter. God was angry once again with the children of Israel for their repeated rebellion and unwillingness to trust and obey Him. As a result, the Lord told Moses that His presence would not accompany the people when they entered the Promised Land. Devastated by God's words, Moses asked the Lord not to send them into the land at all under such circumstances. He further pleaded with the Lord that His presence had to accompany them into the land or it would not be worth going.

The Lord responded in verse 17 by saying, "I will do this thing also that thou hast spoken: for thou hast found grace in my sight, and I know thee by name." The Lord agreed to go with them simply because of Moses's prayer. God's response moved Moses so powerfully that he blurted out, "Lord, please show me Your glory!"

However, after already having a face-to-face experience, what was Moses still longing to see and experience? You would think that there was no greater experience for any human being other than to stand in the presence of God Himself.

After reading this, one day I was in prayer, and I was trying so hard to connect with God the way Moses did. I was saying things like, "God, I want to see You face-to-face. I want a relationship with You like what Moses, Samuel, and Enoch had. O Lord, please let me see Your glory!" Of course, there is nothing wrong with desiring this kind of experience with God.

In many of our church's corporate prayer meetings, we also pray similar things about experiencing the presence of God. Yet one day the Holy Spirit spoke up as I was praying along these lines. I heard Him say, "Moses only dreamed to have what you have!" I didn't quite understand what the Lord meant. "What?" I thought. "How in the world could Moses want what I have?" I told God that I have never seen Him the way Moses did. I couldn't ever remember having an experience quite like the Bible describes about Moses. His life was full of spectacular events. An entire sea split in two right before his very eyes. Sticks were turned into snakes, his face glowed, bushes burned, and water turned to blood. How in the world could he have dreamed to have what I have?

The Lord drew me to Exodus 33 again. After Moses begged to see God's glory, the Lord responded with something different. God did not answer Him with the same type of face-to-face encounter or by another sign or miraculous event. Even though verse 11 records that God talked with him face-to-face, the Lord said later in verse 20 that seeing His full *glory* could not include seeing His face unveiled. Actually, the face-to-face experience Moses had in verse 11 means "to be in the presence of," as if to be in the same room, which is somewhat different from looking directly into someone's eyes or face.

Even with this particular encounter Moses experienced, there must have still been something missing for him to still beg to see God's glory. Moses must have still craved something else, something deeper.

Unable to fulfill Moses's request fully, the Lord responded to him in a different way. God's response here is very prophetic to represent what all of humanity, not just Moses, was craving. As it was with Moses, something is missing. In verse 21, the Lord had Moses perform what was not only a personal experience but also a prophetic act.

He said to Moses, "Behold, there is *a place by me*, and thou shalt stand upon a rock" (emphasis added). God began by showing Moses a prophetic picture of Jesus, who is "the place by God," specifically seated at His right hand. He was the rock Moses was to stand on. In other words, "Moses, the only way you will ever fully know My glory in the way that you desire is through Jesus and what He is about to bring the world."

The story continues in verses 22–23, where we find God placing Moses in the cleft of the rock—the rock of Christ. This was a cavelike area and a "safe place" in which to stand. Yet even though God *wanted* Moses to see the way to His glory, there was something that restrained God from showing Himself fully unveiled to Moses. Still there was a veil, a separation, something incomplete to Moses's desire—even in the "rock" of Christ.

The trouble was that if Moses's physical eyes had seen God without limit, he would have died instantly. Our corruptible flesh just cannot come into contact with God's glory in an unlimited way. He is so powerful that His glory will consume anything corruptible it touches. But we crave to experience God unveiled and without limit in this way. We want to touch Him and see His glory! Even with all his supernatural experiences, it is what Moses knew to be the missing piece.

After I read these verses again and again, I pondered what the Holy Spirit said. "Moses only dreamed to have what you have!" Suddenly I jumped up and said, "Yes, Lord, now I see it." Of course, that was it. Our natural, corruptible flesh cannot see His glory fully unveiled, nor could Moses see it. But God had a plan for us to be able to "see" Him without limit anyhow. It was "in the rock" through Jesus. Jesus enabled us, by His blood, to be able to contain His glory *inside of us* through the Holy Spirit. When the Holy Spirit fills us, we can see Him in our spirit without limit! Your spirit is the place where He is unveiled to you. It is not with our physical eyes because the Lord knows that our flesh would be too frail to handle His power at that level. But our spirits that have been completely changed by the blood of Jesus are able to house His Spirit without measure. It is about connecting to God's glory, Spirit to spirit!

Moses could not have this type of Spirit-to-spirit relationship with God because his spirit had not been reborn in Christ. On the inside, he was spiritually dead, so he could not receive the unlimited glory of the Holy Spirit he desperately craved. Nor could he see it fully on the outside because the glory of God at that level would have killed him. Moses was only left with what he recognized to be an unfulfilled internal craving, so he cried, "Lord, *please* show me Your glory!"

How desperate he must have felt. Each time he walked away from all the wonderful encounters he had with God, he left both empty inside and alone on the outside. No wonder

Moses had to plead with God for His presence to accompany them into the Promised Land! He understood that empty feeling and wanted God's presence even if on the limited, outward level he knew. When he finished talking with God, they were separated until they met again. Can you see it? Based on this, Moses would have dreamed to have what we have.

This Spirit-to-spirit relationship with God was what Adam had before he fell. He carried the unlimited light and glory of God within him. Through the baptism or infilling of the Holy Spirit, we can now receive His unlimited glory within. This isn't to say that we cannot have an outward experience with God, but what good is an outward encounter if you are still empty within? Or what good is an outward encounter if you walk away and are now all alone? Within, you can know Him by revelation, and even though your eyes might be literally looking at the wall in your living room, your spirit is receiving revelation about the Lord that the patriarchs of the Bible could not have known or understood—or felt.

God is determined to reveal His glory to us. He too recognized what Moses found to be lacking in their relationship. By His Spirit, His unlimited glory can bypass the limitations of our corruptible flesh. It is not just about seeing all the miracles, events, and outward encounters as Moses did. Those things are unfulfilling and don't last without the glory, the flow, the river of God working powerfully from *within you*. Remember how easily the children of Israel forgot all the magnificent things God did? Because they lacked the inward revelation of the living God, the outward things didn't have a lasting impact.

Outward miracles and signs are only a small expression of the inward brightness of God's glory you carry.

They are secondary to it. Moses obviously felt the limitation of outward signs and wonders and still asked for the glory. Yet we usually associate the presence of God's glory with these things. However, what God wants us to know is that miracles should manifest from the continuous flow of power from within us, not apart from us. Moses would have given anything to know what that inward river of anointing felt like. He never could experience the supernatural from within.

When I realized this simple fact, that we carry far more than Moses ever did, I could have exploded into shouting at that very moment. It is actually a truth we probably tell ourselves we knew all the time, but honestly, we hardly expect it to manifest in our lives by the way we often talk and pray. We desperately pray and ask for the anointing of Moses, Elijah, or another Old Testament personality we like. We almost talk as if we really missed out on the powerful days of the Bible, don't we? We often respond to our problems as if we are powerless and hope an incredible sign will appear the way they did for Elisha.

Seeing this through new eyes, I looked through my Bible and went to John 4:21–24 where Jesus talked with the woman at the well. I remembered the verses in general, but I hadn't seen them with this revelation before. They say:

> Jesus saith unto her [the woman of Samaria], Woman, believe me, the hour cometh, when ye shall neither in this mountain, nor yet at Jerusalem, worship the Father. Ye worship ye know not what: we know what we worship: for salvation is of the Jews. But the hour cometh, and now is, when the true worshippers shall worship the Father in spirit and in truth: for the Father seeketh such to worship him. God is a

Spirit: and they that worship him must worship him
in spirit and in truth.

While we are always busy trying to connect with God on
an outward level as Moses had to, God is trying to connect
with us in our spirit, because that is the place where you can
know Him without limit! This is where the river of God's
supernatural power flows. It is where His anointing comes to
you. Jesus told the woman at the well in Samaria that there
would come a day when people were not going to have to go
to a physical location to find the river and glory of God, such
as on a mountain (Sinai) or even in Jerusalem.

While Moses and the people of the Old Testament could
only seek God that way, Jesus said plainly that this is not
what the Father is looking for. He is not trying to hold back
the answer to our troubles until the annual prophetic conference or Bible seminar, which would represent our Sinai or
Jerusalem places. Those things will only enhance what God
really wants. What He really wants is a connection right now
in the place you are sitting and reading this book. He wants
a connection inside your spirit because that is what God is;
He is a Spirit!

History Is Changed

Of all of the events in Bible history, there is one special event
that God was waiting for. No, it's not the resurrection of Jesus,
even though that was the event that granted us eternal salvation and a chance to be re-created and spiritually clean.

But even still, God's ultimate plan had not been entirely
fulfilled. Being clean within was not enough to fulfill God's
heart. There was still one other event that was about to change
humanity forever. It was the very thing God was waiting for

and the very thing Moses wanted. It put a clear difference between the Old and New Testaments. After it, people would not act the same way. We would see human beings wage direct warfare with evil spirits. People would speak differently, act differently, and take on a new way about them. They would speak in a strange heavenly language and begin to manifest a new kind of miracles. They would be the kind of miracles dedicated specifically to people's needs, different from the mostly cataclysmic incidents of the Old Testament. What was the event that changed everything? That event was called the Day of Pentecost!

Of all moments in Bible history or thereafter, this one event called Pentecost was God's most fulfilling moment! It was the moment in time when all that man lost in the Garden of Eden was restored. Specifically restored was that God's mighty Spirit, the Holy Spirit, was going to make His home in us, the way He did with Adam. God has never just wanted an outward relationship, as He had with Moses, nor was He ever just looking to give us an outward display of His power. But this is how many of us approach God. We say, "Please, God, show us the miracles." However, we forget one important factor about the miraculous power of God. He wants to show it very much, but He has a specific way in which He wants to display it—from His permanent home inside us out of which the Holy Spirit pours miraculous power. He wants us to pour forth His supernatural power from within.

He is not looking to display Himself from without like the Old Testament. He wants to fill us with that power inside so it is displayed through us. This way we can experience the glory of God everywhere we go and not just at a conference or specific location. Because it is in us, it never leaves us.

Pentecost gave us the ability to be filled to the brim with the river of God so we can display His unlimited power.

God's Fourth Day

The Bible points repeatedly to the powerful Day of Pentecost. Again, I could burst on the inside when I see the prophetic pictures about it woven all throughout the Old Testament. One major example is the vision of the prophet Ezekiel. In Ezekiel 47:1, he saw a river flowing from the house of God. Do you remember that vision? The waters were overflowing and flooding out from under the door. This was a vision depicting God's river of anointing coming out of the church.

We are the house of God; we are His building. (See 1 Corinthians 3:9.) The building Ezekiel saw was the church—both corporately and individually. The river of God, through the infilling or baptism of the Holy Spirit, is overflowing from within you, God's building. The river of God is your source to tap into God's supernatural power.

After Ezekiel saw the waters flowing from the house, he then stepped into direct contact with the waters. It is important to realize that the waters touched him personally. This is what is so powerful about the anointing within: it touches you and moves you as a person. God cares about you as an individual and wants you to feel Him.

In Ezekiel 47:3–5, Ezekiel begins to measure the waters that were flowing and found them at first to be just one thousand cubits deep, which was only ankle-deep water. He measured three more times, and each time the waters were another thousand cubits deeper, rising from the ankles, then to his knees, and eventually to his waist.

Finally, at four thousand cubits, the waters were overflowing and the depth was over his head. At this point, the prophet called the waters a river that could not be crossed over. It means the waters had become very deep and were probably moving fast.

It is from this depth of God's river in you that the Holy Spirit flows. These waters are risky and unpredictable because they flow over your head. That means they are supernatural, because you can't relate to them according to logic. If we want the deep rivers of God, we will have to swim in "over our head" sometimes. That means we cannot approach the anointing intellectually because these waters will flow right over that!

Many people miss the flow of the Spirit because they are too analytical. You can't always figure out the anointing; you have to sense it from your spirit and swim in it. You may not always have all the answers to something lined up in your mind at first, but if you listen to your heart and spend time praying in the Spirit, the Spirit of God flowing in you will lead you to the right conclusion. This is how the river of the Holy Spirit works in you. Allow yourself to step deeper into in the rivers of God where you can't so easily get back to the shore to sort out the pieces and the facts. Start letting the flow that is deep down inside of you take you to new places with the Holy Ghost. That is where the supernatural miracles are!

What also makes the vision of Ezekiel so incredible was that the waters were measured each time in increments of a *thousand*. Numerical terms in Scripture always carry prophetic significance. Specifically, however, the number *thousand* often speaks in terms of single days on God's calendar. So then, one thousand would prophetically equal one day. We see this in 2 Peter 3:8, which says, "But, beloved, be not ignorant of this one thing, that one day is with the Lord as a thousand years, and a thousand years as one day."

Bible scholars say that the earth is about six thousand years old and that about two thousand years ago was when Jesus came. In other words, Jesus came at about Earth's four thousandth year or "fourth day." Pentecost happened around that same time: Earth's four thousandth year.

In Ezekiel's vision, the waters were building each time they were measured, but it wasn't until the four thousandth cubit, or four thousandth year, that the waters began to overflow as a river. I believe Ezekiel was seeing a future event that was about to impact the earth during its four thousandth year. It was the time ordained by God, when rivers would flow from God's house and move out as a raging river. It was the moment in time when the supernatural power of God would fill people!

No doubt Ezekiel saw the pivotal event called Pentecost, the day when God's people would be filled with a river of overflowing power.

Look again at Ezekiel's "four thousand," and see it prophetically as a "fourth day." On the fourth day of Creation, in Genesis 1:14–19, you can also see a prophetic picture of Pentecost through what God created. Each day of Creation carries its own prophetic significance, but on the fourth day, there were three specific elements created. First, the sun and the moon were created, then the stars were created, and lastly day and night were separated from one another. Each of them again points to Pentecost because the creation of the sun and moon represent what Joel prophesied. The familiar passage in Acts 2:16–20 tells us that Pentecost would reveal signs in both the sun and the moon, just as the sun and moon were also unveiled on that day in Creation.

Then the stars are a picture of us—the church. We find it in Daniel 12:3, which says, "And they that be wise shall shine as the brightness of the firmament; and they that turn many to righteousness as the stars for ever and ever." You can clearly see how the stars, or the church, will display the glory of God, just as the stars first did in Genesis. Then finally, when day and night are divided, we see how the Holy Spirit within us made us the light of the world by separating us from darkness (Matt. 5:14). Men and women filled with the Spirit mirror an exact image of what God created on the "fourth day."

What God created on the fourth day and the river that Ezekiel saw with a depth of four thousand cubits show us that God was foretelling the world about the coming event called Pentecost. God must have been looking forward to this special moment! He couldn't wait to fill us with His supernatural power within. There would be signs in the sky, and a river was going to begin flowing from God's house that could not be crossed over. This was the ultimate desire of God's heart. It was to flow right through His people in supernatural power. No wonder God wanted to foretell of this event long before it happened. He wanted people to know that a "fourth day" was coming.

PEOPLE NEED THE POWER

Several years ago, when we first started our church, we went through a season where outside pressure kept telling us to change our Sunday morning service format to a more generic type of ministry. People and other pastors kept saying things like, "You know it is easier to grow a church if you don't offend visitors with too much of that 'Holy Spirit stuff,' because it can scare good people who may not understand it." People strongly encouraged us that we should keep services to an hour or less, with very nonthreatening preaching and literally no move or gifts of the Holy Spirit in operation. Many pastors we knew were really up on the idea. In addition to that, when you have somebody walk out of your church service just after someone receives deliverance or a prophecy takes place, your mind will play tricks on you. "See," your mind will say, "people think your type of church is too radical. People want a different type of church these days. They want a short service with very soft worship and a light message. They don't want to experience God too deeply."

Then you feel you should have an "appeal-to-all" approach to ministry. For a period, that began to weigh on our thinking. You want your church, like any good church, to grow and change lives. Most of us choose these methods really because we want to be good leaders and help as many people as we can. The problem was that there was one missing element we kept noticing with that ministry method—there was no power.

We never really changed our service format, but we sure felt the pressure to do so. Then one day during the Sunday morning service, an anointing for healing just swept through the room. The truth is that the Holy Spirit didn't even give us the option to compromise—the power of the Spirit just kept coming.

That particular Sunday we prayed for some sick people, and there was one particular woman I remember laying hands on. She attended our church regularly, and she really needed deliverance. When I got to her, I had a half thought in the back of my mind that nothing would happen because she never seemed to get any better. She was a tough case! Just as I reached my hand out to touch her, I suddenly saw a batlike creature fly off her chest. I jumped because it startled me. She flew back wildly in a heap and landed on the floor and screamed. It was pretty dramatic. If anything could have startled a visitor, this would have been it.

But there was power in that room because people needed it, and the Holy Spirit wanted them to have it. He didn't seem to care who was visiting or who might be watching that day, just as onlookers were present on the Day of Pentecost. To the Holy Spirit, the personal needs of the people were the most important thing. It is no different today. People need the supernatural power of God. After that day, the countenance of the woman I prayed for had an amazing change. She actually started smiling when she came to church.

On another occasion, we were praying for the sick in another church. It was a smaller congregation. Those who had prayer needs formed a line, and I remember laying hands on one woman who just walked quietly back to her seat after I prayed for her. This one wasn't dramatic at all. Later toward the end of the service, she got up and walked out. Of course, your mind will play tricks on you again, and you assume the person might be offended about something. Toward the end of the service, a group came running in from the back with that same lady rejoicing. They said, "She had terrible kidney stones and was in so much pain, but after the prayer line she went to the restroom and passed them!" This lady felt better and was so happy.

The river of the anointing causes a dramatic change in everyone who will flow with it. What would have happened to those two women had we just decided not to let the river of the Holy Spirit flow out of us because of the pressure of critics? Those ladies might still be suffering. The Holy Spirit wants to unleash His power from the river of your spirit to create dramatic change in situations everywhere you go.

Stories like that always remind me that the river deposited in me through the infilling of the Spirit is always waiting to flow with power. You can't put a price on the joy and smiles on people's faces when they come in contact with the supernatural anointing. If you squelch the river within because of pressure, it will eventually become nothing more than a trickle. Every Spirit-filled Christian has that same river of God available in their spirit, and people are desperate to experience it. We need to increase that flow in our churches again because God's Spirit is in us and He wants to manifest supernatural power. One moment of contact with that kind of power can dramatically change someone forever in a way that natural means cannot. We simply cannot diminish the power of Pentecost, because people need that supernatural dimension of the Holy Spirit now more than ever.

A Dramatic Change in Twelve Men

Pentecost was so pivotal in Bible history that it dramatically changed the disciples of Jesus into new people. Even under the powerful ministry of Jesus, they couldn't seem to get some areas together. In Luke 24:13–31, we find two of the disciples walking on the road just outside of Jerusalem on the morning of Jesus's resurrection. Now they should have been anticipating this day, but instead they were disillusioned and confused. They didn't recognize Jesus when He came near and started talking to them. Verse 16 says, "Their eyes were holden that they should not know him."

When reading this, it is easy to assume that the Spirit of God was the one who was holding their eyes. However, the Bible never says that. The greatest thing holding people's eyes today comes from a hardness of heart or unbelief. We find later in this passage that this is what happened to these disciples. In fact, spiritual blindness is the main product of unbelief. In verse 25, Jesus finally called them fools who were slow of heart to believe. Wow! What a "wonderful" first greeting after rising from the dead! That was obviously a harsh word but nevertheless true.

Their eyes could not recognize Jesus because they were just not expecting Him to show up. In fact, on many different occasions Jesus told them plainly that He would rise from the dead after His crucifixion. Once in Matthew 26:32, Jesus explained that He would go into Galilee to meet them right after He rose. Somehow they missed that statement. Throughout the four Gospels, Jesus corrected them repeatedly for this habit of unbelief. So, when Jesus finally met them on the road in Luke 24, they were so full of this same unbelief that they didn't even know it was Him. The story caps off, in verse 21, with one ultimate comment by one of them who said, "We thought He was *supposed* to have been the Messiah!"

Humorously, these men are just like so many of us. They were afraid of confrontation and persecution; they argued over who had the most powerful ministry and struggled with a serious amount of unbelief. They failed at many miracle attempts and even tried to hide their relationship with Jesus when the pressure was on them.

We can look through these pages of the Gospels and see ourselves. We struggle with timidity sometimes, afraid if we pray boldly for someone's healing that they might die anyway. We think, "What if I try to cast out a demon and it doesn't leave?" There are cases when we are afraid to stand for God because of opposition. This is right where the twelve disciples were. We should be able to identify with them, but the lesson of what God wants us to see doesn't end with identifying with the struggles of the Twelve. The lesson ends with what happened to them later in the Book of Acts.

Something happened to these twelve men that dramatically changed them from timid and unbelieving to bold and powerful. They were transformed suddenly from insecure people into mandated preachers. What caused this incredible difference? It could not have been the resurrection of Jesus, because they struggled terribly with the same issues even into Acts 1:6, when they were still trying to put their own interpretation on Jesus's purpose on the earth. They still believed He was going to take over the Roman Empire and restore power to Israel. This was even after Jesus rose from the dead and had already explained His purpose for coming so many times.

So what transformed them and caused this dramatic change in their lives? It wasn't until a key pivotal event in chapter 2 of the Book of Acts. It was when they were filled with the Holy Spirit that something about them was distinctly different. Peter, who was afraid and who had denied Jesus just a few chapters before, suddenly stood up and preached one of the most confrontational sermons in the New Testament. The same people he had allowed to intimidate him in John 18 he was now holding accountable for Jesus's crucifixion in Acts 2:23.

They left the Upper Room encounter in supernatural power and immediately came to the gate called Beautiful in Acts 3:1–8. They approached a lame man, and Peter said something that is a clue for us to understand what Pentecost literally did for the church. He said three thundering words to the man lying there, and I am sure each word shook every corridor in all of hell! In verse 4, he said to the man, "Look on us." Why were these words so powerful? Because Peter was suddenly confident that something had been deposited inside him. There was a river of the supernatural coming from within him that he clearly recognized. He was telling this lame man to place his focus on what the apostles were carrying in them.

So many of us do not recognize what is actually in us. We might have approached the same situation with the lame man differently by saying something like: "Oh, you poor man. I know your situation is so bad, but just look to Jesus. He will give you the strength to make you feel better about your problem, and maybe He will heal you if He wants." If that man had met many Christians today, he would have never received the miracle. Why? It is not because Peter had more power than we do. Unlike Peter, perhaps we don't fully grasp what has been deposited on the inside in the person of the Holy Spirit.

Peter knew it, and he carried no measure of unbelief about it. Peter didn't even tell the man to look to Jesus. It was not because he wanted to take the focus away from the Lord, but because he knew the Spirit of the Lord was within his own being. Also unlike Peter, we are often afraid to say with authority, "Look on us!" In other words, "We know what we have, because the power of the Holy Spirit is in us and we have come to give you what we have received." Peter told the lame man in Acts 3:6, "Such as *I have* give I thee" (emphasis added). Who had the power? Peter knew *he* had it.

Yes, these twelve men changed dramatically from Acts chapter 1 to Acts chapter 2. Something happened to them. It was called the Holy Ghost and the deposit of the river of God in their spirit. When we were filled with the Holy Spirit, we received that same deposit of power.

This is the very last thing on earth Satan wants you to

know. He absolutely fears everyone who knows it, because he knows that when God's people begin to live from the supernatural well in their spirit, things are about to change. Bondages and bad habits will lose their foothold, healing will manifest, and we will begin to operate in the same power we see in the early church. This is what the Holy Spirit in you wants, and it is what the devil hates. It is the supernatural river of God coming from your own spirit.

PENTECOST: THE RIVER OF POWER

I was ministering in a conference one time, and it was one of those occasions where I knew the Holy Spirit was going to really move. I could sense it. I stood up and preached my message as usual, and then all of a sudden the spirit of boldness hit me. Before I could stop myself, I heard myself say, "I, Brenda Kunneman, have been sent by God to impart into you what is inside me. I have come to take the healing power that is in my spirit and give it to you. If you will take the power inside of you and connect it to mine, it will be like electricity coming together, and miracles will break out everywhere." I didn't have time to even talk myself out of it before the place went wild.

That is why you cannot analyze the anointing; you have to flow with it. I laid hands on the sick, and people were literally being thrown by the power of God. One lady had severe swelling in her legs, and the swelling just went down right there like letting air out of a balloon. People were climbing out of their wheelchairs. I surely must have stepped into a supernatural anointing that day because by the time it was over, I had laid hands individually on over thirty-five hundred people for healing. People were dancing, shouting, and rejoicing. It was almost impossible to end the service.

After that day, I learned something. God told me to begin to declare the anointing that was on me before I minister. I don't always do it publicly, unless I feel directed by the Holy Spirit to do so, but I always do it privately. I prophesy to my spirit and command the supernatural river to begin to flow out of me. That is what Peter did at the Gate Beautiful because he had faith in what was inside of him. Jesus did it also in Luke 4:18, when He said, "The Spirit of the Lord is upon me, because he hath anointed me…" Something will happen when we know who we are and boldly declare who we carry.

This is a key way to get the river of God flowing out of your life for what you need. It will keep your river from dwindling down to a trickle. You cannot live in power with just a trickle. Satan fears raging water, not trickles! Speak aloud about how God has anointed you, for whatever that is, then command the gifts of the Spirit to operate and say that you are sent in the power of the Spirit. You can do this for every situation in life.

Even if you are not called into full-time ministry, you still have a call to be a vessel of light, and you need power to accomplish it. Some may feel declaring who you are in this way appears prideful, and for a select few who decide to cross the line into pride, it might be. But when you know it is the Holy Ghost whose river is in you, then you can speak about it confidently just as Peter did. It is time the people of God are not afraid to say these three words: "Look on us!"

The Bible says in Acts 1:8, "But ye shall receive power, after that the Holy Ghost is come upon you." Here Jesus was preparing His disciples for the event that was about to turn the world upside down. There is something very unique about the word *power*. In the Greek it is *dunamis*, which means "miracles, power, and might." It has one very special characteristic that we often overlook, especially when applying it to ourselves. It comes from a root word called *dunamai*, which means "to make able or possible." In other words, it means the ability to take what was once impossible and cause it to happen through miracle power. Most of us do not have a hard time associating that word with Jesus. He is God of the impossible. Where we have a more difficult time is seeing that kind of power come out of ourselves, and that is the very reason why it doesn't.

Many Christians cannot see themselves doing a miracle, even though they want to. They don't see themselves as conduits of "spiritual electricity." It is easier to see someone else doing the miracle while the devil keeps us focused on our frailties. We look around at our problems that don't seem to go away and forget we carry the anointing of God to deal with them. We think we need preacher so-and-so to help us. Well, we do need ministry support, but we cannot neglect what Jesus said: "*You* shall receive power, when the Holy Ghost comes on *you*." He didn't say someone else; He said *you*.

Do you notice that Jesus never actually qualified what kind of power that was? He just said power. The disciples didn't have to ask Him either. I think they automatically knew because they had watched what real power was for the last three and a half years following Jesus. They didn't even get into a doctrinal debate about it. They just started demonstrating the only example of power they knew; they did what Jesus had been doing.

What has changed today? Nothing has changed. We have received the same power of Acts 1:8. It is the power to do miracles and perform the impossible, not just for other people but even in our own lives. That is where many of us need to manifest the power of God most. The river of the Spirit in you can deal with things. The disciples' terrible habit of unbelief was obliterated in one day when they got a revelation of that power.

What habits and recurring problems do you need the power of God to touch? If you wait for the next church meeting to deal with them, it might be too late. I wouldn't hold off waiting for someone to prophesy to me, even though I would welcome the prophecy if it came. I would rise up and use the supernatural river in my own spirit to begin to flood the problem with *dunamis*. By filling you with the Holy Spirit, God moved you from inability into possibility. Living from the well of your spirit that you received when you were baptized in the Holy Spirit will enable you to walk consistently in whatever you need from God. You are supernatural because the Holy Spirit in you is supernatural.

One Sunday after service, we were at the door of our church and shaking people's hands as they were leaving. God had been really trying to make the point to me about His working power within. One of our newer church members shook my hand as he was leaving, and I went on to the next person. After most people had left, this man came back and called after me as I was turning to go home. He said, "Pastor Brenda, I just had to tell you...when I shook your hand earlier, I felt it jolt me. Power just went into me!" He was so excited. I said, "Really?" Now, do you know that I never felt a thing?

Be confident that if you cultivate the anointing inside of you, it will flow when you don't even realize it's flowing. Have you ever thought how you don't have to "try" to make the electricity in your house flow? You just do what it takes to create the right environment for it. Plug in the appliances, pay the electric bill, and turn on the switch. Then you just forget about it and let the power do its job while you enjoy it. What I realized with this man at the door that day is that the power of God can flow even when you don't see or feel anything. I didn't even try to emit any power. I was just greeting people.

Just start trusting that it is there doing the job just fine, regardless of "feeling" all the time. Don't undo your miracle by the deception that you can't feel anything. The power is in you working and handling it; just keep cultivating the environment for it and expect it to work. That is how the early church walked confidently in so much power. They just expected the supernatural river in them to operate automatically. They *knew* they were anointed!

SUPERNATURAL POWER OR MAN-MADE WATER TANKS?

Not too long ago a family in our church was dealing with a legal situation that was truly not their fault. The devil tried to play an ugly hand through a false accusation. This is a wonderful family in our church who lay their lives down to obey God and grow spiritually in every way they know, and Satan was just afraid of them. Demons like to condemn you and make you feel like a failure right in the middle of your greatest strides of spiritual growth. That was the case with them. When I first heard about what was happening, I began to come up with all the legal fronts they could possibly pursue. In my logical mind of reason, I wanted them to call this person, do that, or say something else—and do it quickly! Sometimes when you're angry, you are ready to go anywhere to pick a fight. That is what I wanted to do.

The following Sunday morning, I told my husband that it was on my heart to pray for them during the service. We called them up, and I was planning to pray a basic pastoral prayer. Then the Holy Spirit shouted in me and said, "Tell them this: '*Nothin' doin'!*'" He wanted them to know there would literally be nothing to worry about because the case against them would not succeed. I guess when the Holy Spirit wants to get a point across, He will prophesy in slang if He wants to. You could just see the chains of fear fall from them. In the excitement of the moment, we all lit up.

When I met with them later in the week, legally speaking, things looked worse. For a moment, I started getting in my head again about the situation. I found myself reverting to talking out every solution I could think of from a natural perspective. After the meeting, the Lord said to me, "What are you doing?" I didn't even answer because I knew what the Lord was going to say. When the Lord asks you a question in your heart like that, it is because He is waiting to hear you say what you already know.

The truth was that I had become moved by the negative circumstances and was starting to put the prophecy on the back burner and concentrate on something else. Now we came up with some good ideas that God used, but the problem was that I ignored the word of the Lord and forgot about the incredible anointing that came with it. Rather than connect my faith to that supernatural occurrence that came in the form of prophecy, it felt more realistic to try a new approach because a feeling of fear was trying to settle in.

After the Lord corrected me, I reconnected my faith to the previous word from God, and I reminded those people of the same. Do you know what happened? The case immediately ended that week with *nothin' doin'!* We have to be so careful that we do not replace the power of God with man-made methods.

MAN-MADE METHODS

Jeremiah 2:13 talks about the danger of replacing the power of the Spirit with man-made methods. It says, "For my people have committed two evils; they have forsaken me the fountain of living waters, and hewed them out cisterns, broken cisterns that can hold no water." This scripture tells us that the people made the mistake of ignoring God, the fountain they were to trust in and rely on. Ultimately, they began to create their own cisterns as a substitute. Cisterns are man-made storage tanks for holding water. These people felt more comfortable with their own manufactured tanks than with God's supply of water available to them. God said their cisterns were broken and could not hold any water. He was saying that their sources of supply were unreliable.

We too can find trouble by creating our own natural solutions to our problems. Rather than trust the fountain of the Spirit within us, we sometimes look elsewhere for quick relief to satisfy our thirst. That can happen so easily if we are not careful. There are a great many ideas and voices out there that can sway a person. But there is one key phrase in the verse above that will help us avoid getting off track. God said of the people, "They have forsaken me." Falling into the trap of creating their own methods didn't come suddenly. It began because the people started ignoring God a little at a time. This was what I did that day with the legal case. It can come on you so easily that you do not even realize you are doing it, which is why we have to be careful. We can unknowingly ignore God and put our eyes on whatever we think will bring us relief right now.

Many Spirit-filled Christians seemed to have lost a degree of appreciation for what Pentecost really gave them. For some of us, perhaps, it is because we never had the full revelation of it in the first place. However, I can also see where the devil has a sly plan to soften the power of Pentecost and reduce its value in our daily lives and ministries. I have learned from warring against the devil that he doesn't like to rob from us in one mass looting. Large demonic attacks that come carrying a big scene usually didn't begin with one. They begin with a series of little distractions and deceptions that pull our eyes off the anointing within. When we choose to bite on it, we veer off course just inches at a time. Then after a series of these same sneaky covert operations by the devil, people eventually find themselves way off base. As a result, the river of God's power becomes virtually nonexistent, and the only answers that feel safe are now birthed from human wisdom. Then people wake up one day wondering where the power went and how they got into such a mess.

When the Azuza Street Revival came over one hundred years ago, there was a massive excitement over the baptism of the Holy Ghost and the gifts of the Spirit. In recent years, however, I have noticed a trend becoming more popular in Spirit-filled churches. Little by little people have replaced their appreciation for the power of the Spirit for other things. It is a trend where people feel safer depending on the word of a secular counselor rather than the river of the Holy Spirit inside them.

Instead of anointing with oil, we feel better about the study of herbs and Internet research on health. Rather than pray in the Spirit and draw God's answer from within, we want to locate a quick opinion that makes us feel good this very minute. Wise natural choices are important, but we have almost begun to give them precedent over the river within, and if we are not careful, we will lose our supernatural spirit. Instead, the river of God should anoint us in such a way that God's miraculous power will give birth to whatever we need, and sometimes it may show us a simple natural solution. We just have to be so careful that we do not let man-made methods replace our dependency on the power of God. Otherwise, we may end up with the wrong results instead of a miracle.

MAKE YOUR RIVER RISE!

By keeping your eyes on the Spirit of God within you and making Him your primary focus, you can pull from that river more easily when you need it. Rivers can recede if they do not continually receive a supply of fresh water. Continually force yourself to stay connected with the anointing. Surround yourself with it and talk about it. It will keep it in the forefront of your thinking and remind you to keep your river full and flowing.

When the early church was undergoing a time of intense persecution in Acts 4:24–31, they did what was necessary to fill up their river so they could keep handling what they were facing. From this passage we can gain four ways that they cultivated God's supernatural power in their lives and kept their river full.

1. They assembled and unified with other believers.

Get around the anointing in other Christians. When people are facing trouble, they often like to run because they are tired of fighting and feel no one understands them. Make yourself go to church regularly, even when you don't feel like it. Stay in unity and refuse to become isolated. Just being in the room with other godly people keeps you focused right. In the long run, this will keep the river of God fresh in your life. The early church was committed to one another.

2. They prayed.

They gathered together in prayer. We can safely assume that they prayed both in their own language and in other tongues as they lifted their voice in unison. Praying in the Spirit is a key part of causing your river to stay full. Consistency in different kinds of prayer and worship will keep you flowing in the supernatural current.

3. They rehearsed the Word of the Lord.

Notice how they went back and recited Scripture and prophetic promises. You have to keep your eyes on the Word of the Lord or you will find another "word" trying to capture your interest. Quote what God said to you again and again, from both the Bible and prophecies you have received.

4. They were bold in the Spirit.

Remember that boldness is a magnet for the anointing. I never like to be quiet about the things of the Spirit. Timidity is an enemy of the anointing. It is like just barely turning on the faucet so the result is a trickle. The early church spoke the Word with boldness, even when it seemed at times to be safer to be reserved about it. As a result they did incredible miracles.

In the end, filling their river levels to full again resulted in the manifestation of God's power. In verse 31, the building shook where they had assembled, and a fresh river poured out from them in full force.

Without question, Pentecost was a pivotal event in history because it changed everything! God was no longer just working outside of people, but He began to flow from within them. Some refuse the power of Pentecost, while others have forgotten what it provides them. The paramount issue is that this wonderful Holy Spirit, who has downloaded *Himself* into our spirits, is more than just a good feeling inside. He is more than a momentary experience at church. He is the all-powerful, unlimited Spirit of God Himself, whose primary desire has *always been* to flow out from within you toward any place where there is a desperate need for living water! Pentecost truly was a pivotal event that changed history.

Chapter Three

DELIVER YOURSELF

MANY PEOPLE ARE seeking deliverance in one form or another. For some, it is deliverance from illness or a financial problem. For others, it is a bad habit or some kind of addiction caused by a demonic stronghold. Additionally, most people also have some personality hangups they need to be delivered from so they can become more Christlike.

The most important thing to know is that the Lord never intended us to travel repeatedly around the same mountains and struggles all our lives. God does not want us bound to the same bad habits, attitudes, sins, negative character traits, or demonic strongholds. Yet many are still bound by them because they do not realize that God planned a guaranteed way for them to break that cycle of failure. It is through learning the secret of self-deliverance.

You may be wondering what that actually means. While we will cover this in depth throughout this chapter, know that it starts with understanding that deliverance begins with you. Those who learn how to use the supernatural equipment inside them will learn how to get free from present bondage and avoid future strongholds. This is how God planned for the church to get delivered from demons and stay free from them. You will also find your healing and provision in the river of your spirit. It is available to address whatever you need in life. That river of supernatural anointing is not only strong enough to address the problem, but its flowing current is also powerful enough to keep impurities from filtering back in.

Remember the power of deliverance comes from within you because that is where the Holy Spirit lives. We can see this in two verses of Scripture. Both are extremely important in understanding how to be free from demonic power.

> But upon mount Zion shall be deliverance, and there shall be holiness; and the house of Jacob shall possess their possessions. And the house of Jacob shall be a fire, and the house of Joseph a flame, and the house of Esau for stubble, and they shall kindle in them, and devour them; and there shall not be any remaining of the house of Esau; for the LORD hath spoken it.
>
> —OBADIAH 17–18

In these two verses, Zion and Jerusalem speak prophetically about the church—the spiritual Israel (Heb. 12:22–23). Jacob represents the Holy Ghost. Jacob was the example of the Holy Spirit just as his grandfather, Abraham, and father, Isaac, represented the heavenly Father and the Son. When you think of both Zion and Jacob, see yourself personally. You are the *spiritual Israel* who is filled with the *Holy Spirit*.

Verse 17 of Obadiah tells us there is one specific characteristic that is visible on Mount Zion or upon your life. Of all the qualities that God could have listed, this one was what He chose above all of them. It is the primary thing God sees when He looks at you. What was that characteristic? It was *deliverance*! When God looks at you, He sees a picture of deliverance. This has been and always will be God's view of His people. The second attribute listed in Obadiah is *holiness*. God sees you completely delivered and holy because His Spirit lives in you.

Maybe that is not how you feel while you are seeing all of your shortcomings and problems around you, but this is what God has determined you to be. The first key to your deliverance is to agree with that. The Lord sees deliverance and holiness when He looks at you, so tell yourself that you are delivered because that is what God has spoken about you.

However, it wasn't just something He said without a good reason behind it. In verse 18, Esau is also mentioned. He represents rebellion and a lost inheritance, because Esau was the man who chose to let go of his birthright (Gen. 25:29–34). He gave away his right to blessing—the way Adam and even Lucifer did. Esau is an example of sin and bondage. His brother, Jacob, however, received the full inheritance Esau gave away. With that understanding, we find that Obadiah 18 says, "The house of Jacob shall be a fire...and the house of Esau for stubble, and they shall kindle in them, and devour them; and there shall not be *any remaining* of the house of Esau" (emphasis added).

It is saying that the fire of Jacob will completely burn away all that is left of Esau. You could paraphrase it this way: "There shall be a fire in the *house* of the Holy Spirit that shall utterly destroy the house of rebellion and lost inheritances." Where does it say the Holy Spirit destroys rebellion? It happens in the *house* of Jacob (the Holy Spirit). That is talking about you—you are the house of God's Spirit!

When you learn that deliverance is already in you, you begin to understand that you carry the power to be free. The fire of the Holy Spirit that lives in you is there to overcome all rebellious activity stealing your God-ordained blessing. God has a good reason to see you delivered because you have the fire of His Spirit on the inside. Is there anything His Spirit cannot handle? He is your source of delivering power so that nothing can keep you bound anymore.

You will be further blessed by Isaiah 62:1–4, which says:

> For Zion's sake will I not hold my peace, and for Jerusalem's sake I will not rest, until the righteousness thereof go forth as brightness, and the salvation thereof as a lamp that burneth. And the Gentiles shall see thy righteousness, and all kings thy glory: and thou shalt be called by a new name, which the mouth of the LORD shall name. Thou shalt also be a crown of glory in the hand of the LORD, and a royal diadem in the hand of thy God. Thou shalt no more be termed Forsaken; neither shall thy land any more be termed Desolate.

Here we find God unwilling to remain silent until the brightness and salvation of the church shines like a burning lamp. God Almighty is on a mission concerning deliverance. The word *salvation* found in verse 1 is the Hebrew word *Yeshua*. This is the name *Jesus*, and His name literally means "deliverance." Jesus died so you could receive His Holy Spirit inside to completely change and deliver you from anything holding you captive. According to this verse, God was not going to stop until that occurred. Notice it says that salvation was like a burning lamp. That fire or burning lamp is the baptism of the Holy Ghost. His infilling in verse 2 caused visible righteousness. It produced glory and a complete name change. He is in you for the express purpose of driving out demonic power. We just need to learn how to utilize what we have.

God was focused on total deliverance when He foresaw the church. He said that He would not rest until He sees it. So when did He finally become satisfied that it happened? It was when the burning lamp or the Holy Spirit came and filled Zion. That is what He was waiting for, so when you were filled with His Spirit, God saw a picture of total deliverance. God just wants to teach us how to tap into what He already knows. It is learning how to tap into the supernatural well of power in your spirit, where the burning lamp dwells. That is the Holy Spirit in you. God Almighty sees nothing else.

THE STALKER IN THE CHURCH

Sometime ago we had an incident in our church that made me realize how much God is devoted to our deliverance. There was a family in the church that had been coming for some time. They had an adult son who came regularly with them, but there was a side to him that left some of the staff feeling uneasy. He did all the right things in front of people. He worshiped God, he was faithful about his attendance, and he talked positively about the ministry. He came from a family of longtime churchgoers. So, as pastors, we couldn't always put our finger on why we felt uneasy about him. At the time, we didn't even communicate to one another about it all that much. There was just something about him.

One night I had a dream that I was in a large building; a number of the church people I knew were there, so I assumed it was a public building or perhaps even the church facility, even though I didn't recognize the backdrop in the dream. I was walking around doing different things and talking to different people as I normally do, but each time I would turn around this young man would appear. He would slide out from behind a door or stand up from behind a bush or something. Every time I looked over my shoulder, he was following me. I began to watch my back in the dream. I started trying to get away from him, but he kept coming. It felt so invading and very wrong.

When I woke up, I told the dream to my husband, and we began to investigate the issue, especially because the father of the young man had by now begun to create another problem in the church. Something was going on, and God was alerting people. Different leaders began to look into the matter. A few days later, we received a call from one of our ministers who runs a mission as an extension of our church. The mission houses several women and children, some who are workers and others who have been saved through that ministry. They reported that this young man had been breaking into their rooms and that they were going to have to contact the authorities. One of the girls said she actually saw him walk into the room at night while she pretended to be sleeping! They found evidence of his trespassing. He began to make phone calls to the women, saying he was watching them. He went so as far to tell them to watch their back because he was always around the corner! It was so creepy!

What he didn't know was that God was watching *him*. People in the church began to be alerted, and after I had the dream, we knew God was going to put His finger on the problem. We confronted the father about the issue he was creating and also the young man about his activities at the mission. They all left the church immediately, and we never heard from the young man again. God was very concerned about our deliverance, but notice how God used the supernatural anointing inside us to alert us to the issue.

On another occasion there was a man (whom we will refer to as Greg) who had been coming to the church for a while.

He seemed nice enough, but again, he kept his distance. He quit coming for a while and then one day started calling the church. He began leaving strange messages on the church voice mail after hours. We assumed he was high on drugs and hallucinating because in the messages he told my husband to quit talking to him and calling him, even though my husband had never called him even once.

This man was also determined that we were following him. His phone messages would stop for a while and then become more frequent. Finally, he started calling and doing the breathing routine on the phone. It became so frequent that one day our receptionist had enough. She is also our head intercessor and a powerful woman of God. She is not afraid to confront a problem if needed. When she answered the phone, she heard the breathing again. Boldly she said, "Greg! I know it's you! Now stop calling right now! We have not been calling you, so good-bye!"

It ended the calls for a short time, but then they started again. However, now the messages became more threatening, until finally we had to call the authorities. One particular Saturday, the man left a voice mail and said, "Pastor Hank, I am calling for you. Wear your black suit to church tomorrow because I am coming after you!" The best we could tell, he was making a death threat.

Perhaps we didn't think he would really show up at service, so somehow we got caught up in the busyness of the morning service and had completely forgotten about the incident. I was standing on the stage while the music was finishing. My husband was still on the front row and hadn't come up yet. I looked toward the back of the church, and this man slipped in the back door wearing a jacket. Now if I responded in the flesh, I would have been tempted to run from the stage screaming, but somehow I kept my head. One part of me didn't want to alert the congregation to anything or get the man to react.

Not sure what to do initially, I prayed in the Spirit under my breath. Then after just a few moments, just as quietly as he slipped in the door, he left. We never heard from him again. The Holy Spirit within drove out the demon that was driving him. God was there for our deliverance, but again it came through the inward anointing.

I learned that if God was committed enough to our deliverance to fill us with His unlimited power so it could expose a stalker and possible assassin, then why is He any less able to destroy the power of personal demonic strongholds in our lives? Isaiah 10:27 says, "And the yoke shall be destroyed because of the anointing." A yoke is a burden or shackle that demons use to control and bind you. However, all binding demon power is subject to that anointing. Bad habits and addictions must also bow to it. Disease and infirmity must bow to it.

In the cases of both the stalker and the assassin, it was God's delivering power that flowed specifically from the power inside believers. It was from the well of Spirit-filled Christians that the plans of the devil were interrupted.

The most important thing to know is that you are able to use the well of your spirit for *your own* personal victories. God wants you to use that supernatural power to deliver yourself. Many people can help someone else get delivered, but they have a hard time walking out their own private deliverance from day to day. They can lay hands on someone else for healing, but they have a hard time walking out divine healing for themselves. But if God would powerfully deliver from dangerous circumstances, as He did for us from the stalker, then how is deliverance for personal issues in your life any different? God has given you the power to be delivered from absolutely anything the devil can throw at you, because the lamp of God's Spirit is burning in you and it contains enough power to force demons out!

DELIVERANCE AND THE NEW TESTAMENT

We may not realize it, but Paul taught extensively on deliverance to the church. He just taught it with a dimension we sometimes overlook. It's not because we mean to overlook it, but as I said before, the last thing the devil wants you to know is what you carry on the inside. He will do anything to keep you from seeing it or remembering it when you need it most. The greatest power on the earth is the Holy Ghost in you!

When obtaining deliverance and ministry for ourselves, the thing we often forget to see is the power within. There is nothing wrong with getting someone else to pray for you and lay hands on you for something. We need that dimension because that is the body of Christ working together to keep one another strong. The Bible says in Hebrews 3:13, "But exhort one another daily, while it is called To day; lest any of you be hardened through the deceitfulness of sin." We need to be there to strengthen each other through our words, through our support, and in prayer. Interaction with other believers also provides accountability, which all of us need if we are going to make it as believers. We need one another. However, there is something along the lines of deliverance, healing, and ministry where Christians and the New Testament are concerned that I want you to see.

Have you ever noticed that after the Day of Pentecost we hardly find any mention of the *Christians* having demons cast out of them? We also find only a few isolated cases of

Christians receiving special ministry from the apostles for healing. Nearly all accounts of this type of ministry were in settings of mostly those who had never encountered Christ. We find Paul cast the demon out of the woman with the spirit of python in Acts 16:16–19, but no real stories like this are written about believers in particular. We do see, however, a great deal of this type of ministry to nonbelievers.

In all of Paul's instructions to the church, he wrote only a small percentage regarding laying hands on one another for healing, and even less about casting demons out of fellow believers. In fact, examples of deliverance ministry toward Christians are virtually nonexistent. The majority of all New Testament scriptures about deliverance ministry surround the persecution of the church and evangelism. Does this mean we ignore the ministry of deliverance for a Christian? No, of course not. If a demon is hanging around, no matter whom he is hanging on, then we had better get rid of him. If someone has opened the door to the devil or been taken advantage of by evil spirits, then we may need to help him deal with the issue, especially if he doesn't know how to do it himself. We as believers can and should help him cast it out (Mark 16:17).

However, there may be an ingredient to deliverance and even healing that we may have forgotten and overlooked. This missing element has led to many of us becoming codependent on counseling sessions, prayer lines, deliverance rooms, and even repeated prophecies to deal with problems and even strongholds. It is because we have developed a habit of always wanting the answers to come from *without* instead of from *within* us. We think if they come through someone else, someone we deem more anointed than ourselves, then we will surely get a breakthrough. Very few have learned the art of depending on the anointing within them to deal with things and that it is a supernatural power. The missing element to your healing and deliverance might be that you have not learned how to pull from the well inside your own spirit.

What we have to consider is that the entire *flavor* of the New Testament seems to point very little to the ministry of sick and demon-bound *believers*. I asked myself the reason for that one day. Inside I pondered a series of questions. Was it because God does not want us healed and set free today? Was it because the practices of healing and deliverance ministry are passed away? I believe those are *not* the reasons at all. God wants every Christian delivered and totally healed. God is devoted to your deliverance. Perhaps the real reason the Bible is not vocal about deliverance and healing ministry toward believers is because God knows how powerful His Spirit is within you. The problem is that many of us don't see it or realize it the way God does, so we don't make a practice of learning to tap into what we carry.

In God's mind, He provided enough power by filling you with Himself. We know that is true because the early apostles functioned that way. They used the power in them to not only live strong but also to deal with the darkness in the world all around them. The flavor of the entire New Testament points to the fact that God already has determined that you are delivered because the fire or lamp of His Spirit is in You. You are the house of the Holy Spirit.

When Paul taught deliverance for believers, he didn't teach deliverance rooms, and he hardly mentions lining up people for prayer during their assemblies. I am sure the apostles ministered to Christians this way some of the time; it is just that the Bible really doesn't draw much attention to it. Instead, Paul seemed to teach total deliverance and abundant living another way. He focused on the fullness of the Spirit within. There is a large New Testament separation between demon-bound nonbelievers and Holy Spirit–filled Christians. Nearly all healing and deliverance ministry was focused on the non-Christian, while the focus for the believer was something far different. Why? I believe the early apostles saw without any shadow of doubt that every believer who is filled with the Holy Ghost possesses all the power they need to get the job done. You can't get any more power to drive out an evil spirit than God Himself.

Could it be that when God's Spirit came at Pentecost that God saw that the source of delivering power for Christians is already housed within them? Yes! God sees His Spirit in you just as you see your car when you fill it with gasoline. Once you have been to the pump, you see your car differently. You know you have the power to get where you are going and do the things you need to do. That is how God sees you full of His Spirit. There is enough power to get the job done.

THE WELL OF POWER IN THE CHURCH

I believe the early church carried a revelation concerning the fullness of the Spirit. It was evident by how they operated in the ministry. They lived and operated from the supernatural well of power within them.

When Paul was attacked by an evil spirit we commonly have come to know as Paul's "thorn in the flesh," God told him exactly how to deal with it. Paul, for a brief moment, was doing what many of us do when assaulted by the devil. We forget the secret weapon that lies within our spirit. Incidentally, Paul's attack by a demon, in 2 Corinthians 12, was not likely a disease, as some have suggested. You can see just before, in chapter 11, that Paul was dealing with numerous attacks of persecution and the heavy load of ministry he carried. The devil was using the trials Paul faced in preaching the gospel to wear him down. I am certain this was the *thorn* that followed Paul—a demon that stirred up trouble every place he went. It was a demon that came to persecute his ministry, trying to hinder him from fulfilling God's call.

In 2 Corinthians 12:7–8, we find Paul asking God to deal with this spirit. Apparently, he was desperate. Then in verse 9, the Lord told him what to do. It was something Paul had in his power the entire time but overlooked it. Verse 9 says, "My grace is sufficient for thee: for my strength is made perfect in weakness." In the Greek, the word *grace* is *charis*, which is the complete favor of God that makes you the recipient of all His benefits. God's favor is *all* that He is, enveloped inside of you. This word also is where we derive the commonly known word *charisma*. In essence, that word means "grace that delivers with miraculous ability." God was telling Paul that His *grace* was enough to handle the problem. The Lord was saying, "Paul, don't you realize that My grace is already yours? It is more than enough to drive this demon away!"

Then the Lord also said, "My strength is made perfect in weakness." God's strength, again, is the word *dunamis*. Here God is talking about His dynamite or miraculous power. He said that His power is only made complete in weakness. Do you know that dynamite only completes its full potential when it is used on something weaker than itself? It is no good to anyone just sitting in the back of a truck somewhere. It is complete and perfected when used on something. It does what it was made to do. God's power is made complete when it is used against whatever the devil uses to be a "thorn" in your side. And we know from the New Testament that this grace is already in us, and it carries supernatural characteristics. God's power is already there to be exerted on your need.

So often, like Paul, we look everywhere for relief, forgetting that the Creator of the universe and His explosive power are residing in our spirits. The answers are all in there! Deliverance and healing are in there. Wisdom is in there. Healing and peace of mind for a broken heart are there, if you are filled with the Holy Spirit. You are lacking nothing that you need to get your breakthrough.

Colossians 2:10 says, "And ye are complete in him, which is the head of all principality and power." Drawing some phraseology from both the American Standard Version and the New Living Translation, you could safely paraphrase this verse like this: "And you are made full (have everything you need) in Christ because He is over every other ruler." Isn't that good? Jesus, in the person of the Holy Spirit in you, has the power to drive out any demon that can bind you because He is the supreme authority.

One of the reasons we don't know this is because the devil tricks us into thinking that we are operating out of a deficit. This is how he tricked Paul. Satan and his demons want you to look inside of yourself and always see a "negative balance" or "insufficient funds." The key for you and me is to know what we have in us and then learn to draw from the abundant power inside.

The truth is you are already delivered by the power in you. Colossians 1:11–13 says:

> Strengthened with all might, according to his glorious power, unto all patience and longsuffering with joyfulness; giving thanks unto the Father, which hath made us meet to be partakers of the inheritance of the saints in light: who hath *delivered us from the*

power of darkness, and hath translated us into the
kingdom of his dear Son.

—EMPHASIS ADDED

This verse says that you have been strengthened with *all*
might that comes straight from *His* glorious power. This is
not just reserved for when we get to heaven someday. See
yourself already delivered from all darkness now, because
it has already happened. The anointing is already in your
spirit to walk it out, and the devil has no ability to hold you
in bondage once you learn how to depend on the power of
deliverance in you.

Now this is not to say that we don't have to walk out our
deliverance. What we need to do is begin that deliverance
process by tapping into the supernatural ability within us.
When you encounter an area of bondage or trial in your life,
you first need to know that God is in you and He wants to
manifest the miraculous through you first and foremost.
Learning to overcome your problems by tapping into God's
grace yourself is the most powerful way to live as a believer.
It will make you an overcomer and a threat to the devil.

HOW THE APOSTLE PAUL
TAUGHT DELIVERANCE

Perhaps Paul's experience with the thorn is why he taught
another dimension of deliverance. It was because the Lord
Himself taught him about his well of supply. While he spoke
very little about the actual ministry of deliverance for Christians and only somewhat more on healing, he did, however,
talk a great deal about living out of the well of your spirit. He
talked about wearing the power of Christ upon you.

The New Testament is filled with these kinds of scriptures.

For your study, below is a list of verses about the *fullness* of the Spirit-filled Christian, and this is only a very small portion of them. You will be amazed at what is already in your life when you read them.

SCRIPTURES AFTER PENTECOST ABOUT THE FULLNESS AND POWER OF THE CHRISTIAN SPIRIT
Jesus tells the church to prepare for dynamite spiritual power (Acts 1:8).
The people were *filled* with the Holy Spirit and spoke in tongues (Acts 2:4).
Peter, *filled* with the Holy Spirit, confronted his accusers (Acts 4:8).
Believers *filled* with the Holy Spirit preached with boldness (Acts 4:31).
Church workers were *full* of the Holy Ghost and *full* of faith (Acts 6:3-5).
Stephen was *full* of faith and did wonders and miracles (Acts 6:8).
Stephen, *filled* with the Holy Spirit, saw a vision of Jesus (Acts 7:55).
The Samaritans received the Holy Spirit and great joy (Acts 8:15-17).
Paul was *filled* with the Holy Spirit and received his sight (Acts 9:17).
The Gentiles received the Holy Spirit and spoke in tongues (Acts 10:44-47).

SCRIPTURES AFTER PENTECOST ABOUT THE FULLNESS AND POWER OF THE CHRISTIAN SPIRIT
Barnabas was *full* of the Holy Ghost and faith (Acts 11:24).
Paul, *full* of the Holy Ghost, confronted the sorcerer (Acts 13:8-12).
The disciples were *filled* with joy and the Holy Ghost, boldly preaching (Acts 13:52).
More were *filled* with the Holy Spirit and spoke in tongues and prophesied (Acts 19:1-6).
Believers are *full* of joy, peace in believing, and hope by the power of the Holy Spirit (Rom 15:13).
Believers are *full* of goodness and *filled* with knowledge (Rom 15:14).
The gifts of the Spirit work in us with the *filling* of the Spirit (1 Cor. 12:11).
Your spirit issues out utterance in tongues (1 Cor. 14:14).
Our inward man (spirit) is renewed daily. It is eternal (2 Cor. 4:16).
Walking fully in the Spirit causes you to overcome fleshly lusts (Gal. 5:16).
The church is *filled* with all Christ's dominion and authority (Eph. 1:20-23).
The power of all God's *fullness* dwells in us (Eph. 3:16-20).

SCRIPTURES AFTER PENTECOST ABOUT THE FULLNESS AND POWER OF THE CHRISTIAN SPIRIT
The *fullness* of Christ brings us to spiritual maturity (Eph. 4:13).
We have the choice to stay *filled* with the Spirit (Eph. 5:18).
We are to be *filled* with the fruits of righteousness (Phil. 1:11).
We are to be *filled* with the knowledge of His will (Col. 1:9).
Christ in you has all *fullness* (Col. 1:19).
Christ is in you, the hope of glory (Col. 1:27).
We are *full* of the assurance of Christ with the treasures of wisdom and knowledge (Col. 2:2–3).
Raised up with Christ, we have all the *fullness* of the Godhead (Col. 2:9–14).
We can walk in the *full* assurance of faith (Heb. 10:22).
Seeing our eternal life with Christ *fills* us with joy (1 John 1:1–4).
The truth of God dwells in us (2 John 2).

I believe not only Paul but also all the apostles made the supernatural well of their spirits the focus for deliverance and the way for all our needs from God to be met. Again, we can see from just this partial list of scriptures that it is the *flavor* of the entire New Testament. They taught living in the Spirit and drawing from the well of the Holy Ghost within.

Paul and his ministry associate Silas knew, when they were locked in a prison cell in Acts 16:23–26, that they could not call for the prayer team or get the conference speaker to prophesy to them at that moment. They had no choice but to draw on the anointing within them. From previous experience, they already knew how to war from the well of their spirits.

If your daily source for a breakthrough always requires the help of someone else, then when you are in a serious situation you won't know how to overcome Satan's power when no one is there to help you. That is how the devil has kept so many people bound. They get all excited after church or after prayer, but by the time they get home, they are already falling back into some of the same old things. They don't know how to live strong and delivered on their own.

Throughout his letters, Paul taught Christians to overcome their bondages, diseases, and other problems by *putting on* the power of Christ. Now that is much more than just gritting your teeth and trying to act as holy, healed, or happy as you possibly can. Instead, it is letting the river of the Spirit flow from you so that you are caught in the wave of a supernatural lifestyle and let it carry you. It is so you can live strong when no one is around, when no one is watching, and when no one is there to pray for you. The devil is most afraid of this kind of deliverance because it has lasting fruit. He knows that a Christian who can live from the power within is unstoppable and will short-circuit his plans every time. On the other hand, the believer who doesn't realize the power he carries will live from struggle to struggle, always trying to look for his next breakthrough.

This is the reason the apostles didn't focus teaching on prayer lines or deliverance and counseling rooms to help the churches. They taught them how to depend on the Holy Spirit's power within them to destroy the works of darkness themselves.

SIX STEPS TO DELIVER YOURSELF

Isaiah 52:2 says, "Loose thyself from the bands of thy neck, O captive daughter of Zion." Who does this verse say should do the deliverance? You should do it. So here are some steps you can take to cause the supernatural river in you to deliver you—permanently. These simple steps will cause the river in your spirit to start flowing freely, and they will blanket any stronghold with supernatural power. This supernatural power will drive demons out.

1. **Study it.** Get full of Bible truth regarding the fact that you are full of God's supernatural power. Also study scriptures that deal along the lines of your specific issue. Revelation will produce the power of faith from within you. Second Timothy 2:15 says, "Study to show thyself approved unto God, a workman that needeth not be ashamed…"

2. **Know it.** Know what you are dealing with and face it. Call it for what it is, and perhaps even write it down on paper. Then accept what God has to say about it and hold on to that truth. John 8:31–32 says, "If ye continue in my word, then are ye my disciples indeed; and ye shall know the truth, and the truth shall make you free."

3. **Speak it.** Start talking about how you have the power to overcome it. Do this not only when the pain or pressure of it is not on you, but especially when it *is* upon you. The more you speak deliverance, the more it will solidify in you. Declare that you are an anointed vessel of God, well able to drive the demon or problem out. Command the problem to be removed from your life. Matthew 21:21 says, "But also if ye shall say unto this mountain, Be thou removed, and be thou cast into the sea; it shall be done."

4. **Pray it.** Spend some time every day in prayer about it. Talk to God in faith and with confidence, mixed with a contrite heart. Pray in tongues every day because this is such a powerful key to the supernatural! Luke 22:46 says, "Rise and pray, lest ye enter into temptation."

5. **Resist it.** Avoid things you used to do that caused you to fail or feel discouraged. Change habits, locations, schedules, and relationships that pull you down. Replace evil with good, negative with positive. Also tell the stronghold to leave in the name of Jesus. James 4:7 says, "Submit yourselves therefore to God. Resist the devil, and he will flee from you."

6. **Connect it.** We all need to be connected with other believers, not so they can do our deliverance, praying, and spiritual work for us, but so the anointing in them can draw out the anointing in us. Proverbs 27:17 says, "Iron sharpeneth iron;

so a man sharpeneth the countenance of his
friend.”

These six things will cause the supernatural river of God's
power to manifest on the powers of darkness, if you will be
consistent with them. You may be saying, “But these things
don't seem very supernatural!” However, it is often through
the things that seem the most ordinary that the supernatural
power is released. In fact, that is how God usually works.

Do you remember the story of Naaman in 2 Kings 5? He
was a warrior for the king of Syria, but the problem was that
he was a leper. You could say he needed deliverance! When
the king heard that the prophet Elisha was in Israel, the king
decided to send Naaman the leper to the prophet so he could
be cured. When Naaman came to Elisha, the prophet told
him to wash in the Jordan River (2 Kings 5:10). Naaman
became furious at the prophet's request because he felt the
prophet's planned steps for his deliverance were too ordinary. In 2 Kings 5:11, Naaman said, “Behold, I thought, He
will surely come out to me, and stand, and call on the name
of the LORD his God, and strike his hand over the place, and
recover the leper.”

In addition to that, we find in verse 12 that Naaman was
also angry that the prophet had not only asked him to do
something ordinary like wash in a river, but that he even
picked a dirty river instead of some of the nicer ones in
the region. Naaman wanted the prophet to do some great
spectacular thing, but instead he was expected to wash in
a muddy river. He didn't realize that one ordinary, seemingly mundane, and pointless step was going to release the
supernatural.

What would happen if every day you would just follow the
six steps listed above? You would find that the river of the

supernatural God has placed in you would start to flow and bring a miracle to solve your issues. If Naaman had refused to take those steps, the power of God available wouldn't have been released to help him.

Learning to deliver yourself through the river of God in your own spirit begins with simple steps that at times may seem insignificant, but they are the very thing that will release the power of God to you. They stir the anointing.

A WOMAN, SOME DEMONS, AND A SPIRITUAL WELL

A wonderful and anointed woman of God in our church is a walking testimony to self-deliverance from the well of her spirit. She came to our church many years ago completely bound under the weight of evil spirits. Her mind was so abnormal that many psychologists and doctors did not know how to help her. They diagnosed her with severe bipolar disorder and borderline personality disorder. She would complain of seeing graphic visions of cutting her own throat, and she abused drugs and alcohol to try and kill herself on a regular basis. She would suffer from cycles of severe depression, fits of rage, and bizarre behaviors. She would sometimes just cry uncontrollably for days. Doctors were baffled with how to help her. No medications cured her, and they had come to the point of wanting to administer electroshock therapy as a final resort.

When she came to us, her countenance was so dark, and we could see the presence of evil spirits on her. We had seen times when she seemed to be a very normal person, but then the demons would manifest themselves. And even though we knew she had gotten saved and filled with the Holy Spirit shortly before visiting our church, it was obvious to us that she was still bound. She knew very little about the power of God back then, but she desperately wanted to be free. We finally met with her for deliverance.

Our deliverance meeting with her was an amazing event. When we began to command the demons to come out of her and loose her in the name of Jesus, the demons wanted to speak out. My husband told them to be silent! She told us later that she felt like someone stuffed cotton in her mouth. We took authority over every spirit binding her. She said, "I have never felt so much physical pressure on my body, and although I don't remember for sure, it seemed like I lifted off the ground and something departed from me."

After we prayed, she looked lighter and was actually smiling. You could see that she was different. Something *did* leave her—it was evil spirits. However, when she left the deliverance meeting with us, she was still taking medications. She seemed much better, but still not everything was completely right. The evil spirits were not going to stay away easily.

Now this is the part of deliverance from the well of your spirit I want you to see. This is where most people either walk out their deliverance fully or go back to bondage. This is why your breakthrough cannot be found only in laying on of hands, counseling, or a deliverance meeting. You have to do something, and it must come from the anointing within *you*. She told me later, "I had to walk out a process in my own deliverance. I had to retrain my mind how to live normally because I did not know how to do that without depending on these spirits. I was tempted many times to go back to the way I was."

One day she said, "Pastor Brenda, I seem to feel better. I want to quit taking my medicine and trust God, but I am not sure what I should do." Now, as a pastor, I *never* advise

anyone to quit taking their medication because that is something they have to choose under the care of a doctor. However,
I told her to make some simple, seemingly ordinary steps. I
told her to begin by taking a dose of God's Word every time
she took a dose of her medication. I told her to put note cards
with Bible verses written on them next to the pill bottles and
declare aloud a "dose" of Scripture along with the dose of the
prescribed medicine. She told me she did it faithfully every
time. I gave her specific scriptures to speak over herself.

As a result, something powerful started happening. After
a while of doing this, she decided to visit with her doctors
about coming off her medicine. She told them that she
believed God had healed her and that she wanted to quit her
medications. They begged her not to do it because they felt
that if she kept going, she might be close to a breakthrough.
However, she *knew* that she was healed because every day she
made the simple step of "eating" a Bible verse, and she was
starting to feel the tangible power of God.

Determined she was healed, she eventually chose on her
own to quit her medications—I didn't advise her to do that.
But do you know what happened? She quit her meds, and
she experienced no ill effects from stopping her pills. The
anointing had taken the lead! She also came to church every
time the doors were open and began to learn about the well of
power within her. She stayed in close contact with the church
family and was open about her testimony. The anointing on
the church and the people in it began to pull the anointing
out of her. She also said, "I began praying in tongues every
time my mind wanted to revert to bondage. I would pace and
speak those scriptures again." She renewed her mind every
day with those verses and crucified the desires of her flesh

by speaking to them and commanding them to obey the anointing. She resisted the devil.

She told me that she had to do this for quite some time, even after her deliverance. It was a process, but she began to do these simple steps, and in turn she released the supernatural power of the Holy Spirit. Her daily choice to do the things that release the power of God kept her free.

The greatest lesson we can learn from her deliverance story is when she said, "Even though I had been saved and Spirit-filled, I didn't realize the power was in me to be free. Before, I would just try to feel different and try harder to get better because I wanted to be a Christian, but nothing worked." Then she said, "I felt the demons leave when we prayed, but I quickly realized that I had to retrain myself how to live. I did it with the power of the Holy Spirit in me." Today she is an anointed woman of God and has a testimony of deliverance that came from the well of the Holy Spirit in her. She is medication free and one of our greatest prayer warriors in the church. Thank God for His power!

Leviathan Is Broken

Many years ago we dealt with a situation where we had to depend on the well of anointing within. As many ministers know, not everyone who visits or even attends your church will end up being your biggest fan. A person may begin as a friend and ultimately become an enemy. In one case, an individual attended our church whose family seemed friendly at first but eventually became very angry about the church. The family was really upset and did everything possible to discredit the ministry. They wrote horrible e-mails about us, our ministry, and our character. They even went as far as to hire a man to act like some kind of "heresy hunter," so to speak, to create lies and other rumors about the church.

I have found with some people that no matter what you try, they will never see your heart that wants to do right by them. The scenario got even worse when this family called a particular large, nationally known secular institution they were connected to, stating that we were a terrible cult and that we were trying to "brainwash" their relative. The institution they called is one whose roots are found in humanism and pride. Leviathan is found in pride. He also uses false accusation to exalt himself. We really felt that an evil spirit of Leviathan was released against our church.

The false accusation against our church by itself would not have been so bad, except that this institution took an interest in the accusation of this family and actually called us on the phone. They now wanted to investigate our credibility! Before this, we had prayed about the situation, but by this point it was spiraling out of control, and the pressure began to be overwhelming.

After this institution called and began to question the legitimacy of our ministry, they demanded our tenets of faith and wanted us to take psychological examinations. We could not believe what was happening. At the time, we felt helpless. We tried to cooperate in effort to be considerate and professional. We did everything we knew to handle the problem, but it just seemed to keep getting worse.

Then finally one day we realized our natural efforts were not helping. We needed to take serious action in the Spirit now. These were outright lies and we were tired of them, so we directed our attention on the devil and began to deal with the situation in the Spirit.

One night at home, we rose up and began to pray loudly

in the Spirit. We commanded this demon to stop, and we broke the spirit of pride and humanism that was falsely accusing us. We commanded the mouth of the accuser to be bound in the name of Jesus! We also told our minds to come into submission to the power of Christ and told our flesh to respond in faith instead of fear. Even though we had prayed about it before, this time our prayers were different. We came with an attitude that we were anointed! There was a flow in it. It wasn't mousy prayers anymore. It was the kind of prayer where you know who you are and what you came to accomplish. That night we only actually prayed for about thirty minutes, but it was one fiery half hour. We could feel the river of God flowing out of us this time.

Do you know what happened? Immediately God began to intervene, and just a few short months later, nearly every person on the staff of the institution accusing us was released from their positions due to another unrelated issue. It was all over the news. The result was that they completely forgot about us and the situation was over. The heresy hunter disappeared too.

God delivered us, but it took us rising up and using the well of power we had on the inside. This time we reminded ourselves that *we were anointed* and had the power to stand against the devil. When we tried to fight it by natural means, the matter just got worse. But when we realized we had the anointing to deal with it and we rose up in that position, the supernatural power of God was released, and it broke the back of that attack.

How to Experience Deliverance in Three Realms

Earlier we talked about how rivers have different tributaries that touch different places the main river cannot. It is the same way with the river of the Holy Spirit in you. The rivers of anointing that come from you can be tailor-made to deal with certain problems. There is not a problem you can experience that the anointing will not touch. The Spirit within you is available to touch every part of your being. The power of the Holy Spirit within you needs to touch three realms of your life for you to be totally delivered.

1. *Your spirit*—the salvation/new-birth experience

Your spirit is your inward man that was renewed when you were born again. Second Corinthians 5:17 says it has been completely rebuilt. The old has been taken away and your spirit was made brand-new in one moment when Jesus became your Lord and the Holy Spirit filled you. The deliverance of your spirit is instantaneous in nature, and demons immediately lose their territory in your spirit through the new birth. The results are seen in the way your heart becomes suddenly hungry for God and you are now drawn to Him and His ways. Once your spirit is delivered through the new-birth experience (John 3:3; Rom. 10:9–10), God fuels you with His power through the baptism of the Holy Spirit (Acts 1:8; 2:4, 38–39). It is the power you need so that not just your spirit but also the other parts of you can experience the same delivering power. It is when God downloads His river of anointing into you to begin addressing the trials of life.

2. *Your mind*—the walking-in-the-Spirit experience

The battleground of the mind is the place that keeps many people bound, even though they have the power to be free. People do not stay bound because they don't want to see themselves free in their thoughts, nor is it because they don't try hard enough to think pure and do the right things. It is because a lifestyle of certain patterns and demonic strongholds leave a permanent imprint on their minds. It is similar to the way computers create "footprints" for things that have been typed before, like a Web site or e-mail address. A pattern is created.

Without the power of the Holy Spirit dealing with the footprints in your mind, you will return to the same responses when the pressures of life push your buttons the right way. You will "fill in" the respective need automatically with a previous habit or response, not always even aware you are doing it. Some people turn to addictions or substance abuse; others turn to anger, lying, or control tactics such as hurtful words or the silent treatment. Still other footprints people use to respond to life's pressures are fear, bad eating habits, laziness, or gossip. While demons can be behind these behaviors, you will not be fully delivered unless you deal with the footprints in your mind. I like to say it this way: you can chase away the flies, but you still need to heal the wounds! Most of these footprints were created by demons using other people to hurt you and then leaving its scars behind. Often they come by the way we were raised and patterns that were formed from it.

Your mind is very complex and has five parts to it—your will, intellect, emotions, imagination, and memory. Every part of your mind needs new footprints created to erase the ones left behind by the evils of this world. Even if you cast demons out of a person, that individual still needs to retrain his or her mind's eye and lifestyle to see and experience something new. Your mind has trained itself to tell your body what to do to handle a situation.

The only way to be delivered from the darkness in your mind is by renewing your mind according to Romans 12:2, which says, "Be not conformed to this world: but be ye transformed by the renewing of your *mind*" (emphasis added). How does it say you are transformed? When your mind is renewed. Renewed from what? The previous footprints created by sin and the world. The deliverance of your mind is *a gradual process* as you allow the river of the Holy Spirit to deal with different areas of your mind. You do that by exposing your mind to spiritual things regularly. Let the waters of the Spirit make contact with your mind by revolving yourself around the Lord.

Your mind is caught between your victorious new spirit and your old mortal body. It is the referee between the two. Demons lose their footholds on your mind as the flow from your spirit deals with each area, one by one, allowing your new man to dominate. The fruit of a delivered mind is seen when you address it by *walking in the Spirit* according to Galatians 5:15–17. Walking in the Spirit means that you choose to do spiritual things so that you will not fulfill the desires of the flesh. Then when life's pressures press your buttons, you become retrained not to respond to an old footprint. That footprint is eventually deleted by the power of God in you!

3. *Your body*—the daily crucifixion experience

The Bible teaches us that our bodies are on a course toward death. In 2 Corinthians 4:16 we see that "...though our outward man perish, yet the inward man is renewed day by day." Our mortal bodies will all die someday, and it is easy to tell. We have to remind them to fight against pain and illness. Have you ever noticed how much you would rather sit on the couch and eat potato chips than run on the treadmill? I would! That is because our bodies are happy to sit and do nothing but go down with the ship! Your body is consumed with pleasure and comfort, even if it has to sin in order to feel it. It also struggles to keep up the fight against sickness and disease. The Bible says our flesh is directly opposed to our reborn spirit. It will fight to get whatever it wants to enjoy.

Getting your body to fight its desire to sin and die is the greatest battle of the Christian. We need the supernatural power of God to pour from our spirit and renewed mind for it to be delivered and set free. Deliverance for your body or flesh is a daily choice of crucifixion. That means your fleshly desires and comforts need to be placed upon their own cross and crucified. You can read about the crucifixion of the flesh in Romans chapters 6, 7, and 8. Galatians 2:20 says, "I am crucified with Christ: nevertheless I live; yet not I, but Christ liveth in me: and the life which I now live in the flesh I live by the faith of the Son of God, who loved me, and gave himself for me." This verse gives us some golden nuggets to walking in deliverance in our body: (1) Making the daily choice that it is not what I want but what Jesus wants (that is daily crucifixion), (2) actively using faith and God's power for your deliverance, and (3) knowing that God loves you unconditionally and is giving of Himself for you to be free.

Each of these applies not only to the desires of your flesh but also for your physical healing. They will work to deliver your body in every area. The *result* and fruit of your flesh being delivered are seen when the same desires, lusts, pains, and illnesses don't tempt you and hurt you the way they once did.

ABUNDANT FREEDOM FOR YOU
IN PERSONAL VICTORY!

Like the wonderful woman I mentioned earlier who was delivered, you too can walk in the power of God in your own life that way. My own greatest victories have been experienced privately by using my own anointing within me day to day. This is the deliverance that lasts once you learn how to live in it. It is not just trying harder or living your best, even though that is important. It is taking the things of the Spirit inside you and working and using them to eradicate bondage and disease with supernatural power. Those things within you from the Holy Spirit are powerful to correct the problem if utilized. You don't have to make them work; they will do the job if you allow them to work by doing the things that release them.

For example, if you want to wash the sink, then it is as simple as just turning on the faucet. You don't have to try to make it work; you just turn the handle and let the water flow out and do the rest. Most people try to wash their spiritual sink by getting water from someone else's bucket all the time, or they try some other method to clean out the dirt. Just turn on the faucet of the power of God. It may take some time to do the cleaning, but don't quit; keep the water running! It will work for any area you are struggling to overcome. That delivering power will wash away disease. If you want to be free, be healed, and receive your inheritance of blessing, then let the anointing flow from inside you. Don't worry about how the results look the first day. Just keep the power working, and eventually you will find every speck of darkness washed away.

Consistency will create momentum and an atmosphere where God's power can build. By allowing the anointing within to lie dormant, you may miss the best God has for you and find yourself accepting second best or always needing to depend on others to bail you out of things.

If the apostle Paul could obtain it, if the woman with bipolar disorder could have it, and if the early church could enjoy it, then you can too! From the well of anointing within, you can live delivered in ways that you have never even dreamed possible.

Take it from a man who knew. Paul said in Ephesians 3:20, "Now unto him that is able to do exceeding abundantly above all that we can ask or think, according to *the power that worketh in us*" (emphasis added). He realized that if he was going to escape the power of demons, he was going to have to work with the grace God put in him through the person of the Holy Spirit. He was going to have to use the powerful tools placed in him. God wants you free the exact same way, and He has made provision for you to do it. His power in you will do more than you dreamed. You will know your greatest, lasting victories when you use the supernatural power from the well of your spirit to deliver yourself.

Chapter Four

YOUR SUPERNATURAL SUPPLY

I T WAS IN the middle of the noonday heat, the kind of hot
weather where your mouth feels so dry it is almost difficult to swallow. Just a small drink, a sip of cool water,
was all He was looking for, or was He looking for something else? Traveling through Samaria, He came to Jacob's
well. Not just any well, but the one specifically located in a
land that Jacob received from his father, Isaac. After a long
morning of travel, Jesus walked through Samaria just to get
a drink of water because He was tired from the journey. He
was all alone because the disciples had left to buy some food.
Looking for water, He sat on Jacob's well.

Then she came to the well, the Samaritan woman. In those
days, the Jews considered Samaritans the lesser racial class.
The Samaritans were part Jew and part Gentile, and Jews
didn't do business with them. So there was Jesus, a Jew, and
this Samaritan woman at the well. It was obvious that she
had been through a lot in her life. She carried that look of
someone who had suffered the pain of repeated rejection just
trying to find love. As always, she came to draw the daily
supply of water. She carried not only the water pots but also
the hurts that the burdens of life had brought her. She had
tried everything she knew to feel happiness.

Then she saw Him sitting on the well. Immediately, Jesus

asked her for a drink of water to cool His thirst. "What?" She thought, "This man is a Jew. How could he want me to give Him water?" It was an unusual request, so she repeated her thoughts to Him. "Sir, how could you ask me for water? I am a Samaritan!" This man was different somehow, but she couldn't place her finger on what it was. His reply to her was not an ordinary answer either, and she wouldn't know that it was meant for not only her. It had to do with the river of God, not the actual physical water from that well. It was about spiritual water. He didn't just come to Jacob's well for a natural drink, but it was to tell us about a spiritual drink that we can depend on to be our source of supply every day.

The End of Yourself

This story, which we often know as "The Woman at the Well," is found in John 4:6–30. It was no accident that Jesus chose this well above all the others that were probably available. Of all the places He could have stopped for a drink, He stopped here. This was Jacob's well. Who was Jacob? Remember that he was a type of the Holy Spirit. Jesus chose this well in particular because He was about to paint a picture of the coming Holy Spirit and His flow of power from within. On this day He began to tell it to the Samaritan woman.

It all occurred right about the sixth hour of the day, a very prophetic hour. Jesus never does anything by accident; He came at that exact moment in time. The sixth hour was so important because six is the number of man. During Creation, the sixth day was the day when man was created. Six represents man's methods, man's ideals, and man's own natural wisdom. The sixth hour was about noon; it was the heat of the day. Jesus purposely wanted to visit Jacob's well during a time of day that represented man's own effort, which produces little results and leaves us thirsty and dry in the heat of life.

This woman came during the heat of the day, bearing her own set of trials. She had been married five times, and now she was living with a man to whom she was not married. In her *sixth* hour and *sixth* relationship, she had reached the end of human hope. It is no doubt that she was at the end of her own rope, her own effort to fulfill herself. Nothing had been working up to now.

Coming to the end of your own rope is when you realize the things you have depended upon are leaving you without any fulfillment or answers. Whether it is in relationships, physical health, financial planning, or other personal things, we will eventually come to the end of ourselves. We can't do it our way, because, like this woman from Samaria, our way will fail us. We will eventually find ourselves right where we began, only this time with a longer list of frustrations, hurts, and disappointments. The best thing is to come to the end of yourself so you can begin to receive a new source of fulfillment and support from the Lord. It is more than just knowing God is there for you and trying to allow that concept to make you feel better. It is depending on an active source of power from the Spirit of God to move on your behalf and change circumstances. The only dependable way is through the continual supply of the Spirit.

GIVE THE LORD A DRINK FROM YOUR WELL

Jesus creatively taught this woman how the supply of the Spirit is so much better than our natural efforts. In John 4:7, He asked her to give Him a drink of water. She was a Samaritan, and not only did she feel socially unacceptable to provide the water, but she almost seemed to respond in jest.

She said, "Sir, how is it that you are asking me for water? I mean, come on, you know Jews don't work with Samaritans that way! I can't be giving water to you!"

But Jesus's answer in verse 10 is amazing. It is almost as if He was expecting her to say that. He said, "If you knew the *gift* of God..." In other words, He said, "Woman, if you could just understand what is about to be made available and what I am going to make possible for you, then you would be begging for a drink. Once you drink of spiritual water, *you* could easily supply the need for anything or anyone who asks for that kind of supply from you. The water I am going to give will provide everything. It will answer every problem, and you can use it to help not only yourself but also others."

He was presenting her with a source that would meet her every need both physically and spiritually. He was saying the same thing that Peter later offered to the people in Acts 2:38, "...and ye shall receive the *gift* of the Holy Ghost" (emphasis added).

Jesus deliberately asked *her* to provide the water, knowing that as a Samaritan she would question her ability to do so. He was using her feeling of natural inadequacy to show her a spiritual truth. He wanted her to see that in her present condition she could not supply the need. This is where many people are, even Christians. We are trying to provide for our needs without the power of living water. Suddenly Jesus helped her realize that the gift of God could change all that. It could completely change who she was and bring her from lacking in everything to being able and well supplied. It could fulfill her life *and* change her present circumstances. The Lord wanted her to see the power of living water so she would immediately see that her own ability could not relieve the heat of her sixth hour.

She did exactly what Jesus was looking for: she saw that she couldn't supply the need, so in verse 15, she says emphatically, "Sir, give me this water." She knew she needed a new source! Like all of us, she had to come to the end of herself and draw from the power of living water. Today, because of the baptism in the Holy Spirit, you and I have that source of supply. We have to look to the Holy Spirit within and draw from Him.

What help are you looking for in the middle of your sixth hour? Are you drawing from the well within? Are you willing to give the Lord a drink from your well? You can look within and draw out the answers to deal with the heat of your sixth-hour thirst. The Lord wants you to draw from your well of living water and give Him a drink. He wants you to pull from the supply you have inside of you.

The Vision of Stripes

Of course, when you are in the middle of a sixth-hour trial, everything tries to keep you feeling insecure about depending on the anointing and drawing from it. There are doctor's reports, news reports, financial reports, and more, all of which are saying something different. Sometimes they paint a discouraging picture of tomorrow, making you frantic about what to do.

Years ago, we had such a situation when my father was in a coma. The doctor thought that he was on his deathbed. He suffered septic shock and renal failure so severe that the doctors had no record of anyone who had lived through such an ordeal. He had been in that condition for almost a month. As a family, we were drawing from our well in every way we knew. We prayed, we spoke the Word of God, and we stood our ground. The Spirit of the Lord was faithful to provide each of us special and unique words that we depended on. We each had different scriptures that were our personal *rhema* word from the Lord.

However, I had one experience that settled the answer for me. I specifically remember praying one night. I said, "Lord, I have prayed and trusted Your Word. I have asked that You allow my father to live. I need Your power to work now!" I began to quietly pray in the Spirit and then closed my eyes to go to sleep. As I prayed in tongues, I just put my focus on the Holy Spirit and His power. I was really just trying to turn my thoughts away from the mayhem of fear that tried to intimidate all of us every single day. Exhausted, I just lay there as the utterance of the Spirit rolled from my mouth. I didn't want to read another scripture. I just wanted the Holy Spirit to know I needed Him, because none of us could do this on our own. I remember being tired, dozing in and out of sleep, and then I saw Jesus.

He walked into the dimly lit hospital room with machines everywhere. I cannot tell you if I actually saw Him with my physical eyes or if I had a dream; it was so real! However, when it happened I was originally in my hotel room and then in the hospital room at that moment. Jesus walked over to the patient's portable table normally used for eating, which had my father's medical records sitting on it. The Lord knew I was watching Him from across the room on the other side of my father's bed. The record book was a three-inch loose-leaf binder crammed with medical reports. There were also other folders and papers; the table was filled with these reports. Jesus walked directly to them and looked down at them. He was wearing a long white tunic that tied around His midsection and draped across his chest. It attached at both shoulders with what looked like some kind of gold clips.

Standing in front of the tray of medical papers, He slowly turned around with His back facing directly at the table. Two angels reached up to the gold clips on each shoulder, and when they did, the clips came loose, and the tunic He wore dropped until it was now only around His waist and hung to the floor. His entire back was bare, and I could see that it was covered with scars. He looked up again over His shoulder at the medical records with His back directly facing them. I knew what He was doing. He was showing me that His stripes paid for the diseases written on those reports. His back was pointed at them according to Isaiah 53:5: "But he was wounded for our transgressions, he was bruised for our iniquities: the chastisement of our peace was upon him; and with his stripes we are healed."

Jesus wanted me to know that He received those scars so my dad could be healed. I realized that it was not in how hard all of us tried to make Dad's healing happen; we just had to trust the anointing and that it was in fact working. Shortly thereafter, among many other testimonies my family members all experienced, my dad began to turn for the better. In less than one month, he was awake and eating pizza and Popsicles! Today he has none of the ill effects doctors said he would have if he even lived at all. The vision of the stripes was the personal turning point for me. It was the moment when I was finally certain that the job was done, not based on the medical reports, but based on the fact that God reminded me in that vision that His power was very much in operation. Up to that point, along with my family I had prayed, prophesied, and stood for my answer, but this experience was different. I believe the difference that day was when I finally came to the end of myself and trusted God's power. I resolved to trust God that the supernatural power was working regardless of what it looked like. I am convinced that somehow in that moment my Jacob's well of supply took the lead. Instead of trying to make the power work, I finally trusted that it *was* working.

I wish I could give an exact principle to help you reach that point in your own trials, but I can't exactly. How to walk in the supernatural cannot always be explained, because it isn't natural. What your well-of-the-Spirit experience provides you may be different from mine. It ought to be, because the Spirit of the Lord tailor-makes the water to flow uniquely over you in a way that is special to your situation. That is why drawing from your own well is so vital! You just have to fall into the river by praying in the Spirit, giving yourself to the Lord, and then letting the current of anointing take over. You don't always know where it will take you, but it will always be what you need. It will finish the fight for you.

The "Never-Thirst-Again" Experience

You will know that living water has washed over you when you have what I call a "never-thirst-again" experience. Again in John 4:13–14, while talking with the Samaritan woman, Jesus said, "Whosoever drinketh of this water shall thirst again: but whosoever drinketh of the water that I shall give him shall never thirst; but the water that I shall give him shall be *in him* a well of water springing up into everlasting life" (emphasis added). He was saying that God's plan is for every person to come to a place where they are totally satisfied and feel like their thirst for God or need for Him to do something is settled. Their thirst for God to answer their prayers is satisfied regardless. Satisfaction in life is more than just the fulfillment you received when you got saved and filled with the Spirit. It is something God wants you to experience in every situation. It means that you don't deal with daily circumstances wondering if God forgot about you. Many Christians feel this way, which is the reason they grasp desperately for answers from whatever sources they can, many of which don't include God at all. Sometimes we are concerned that God may not come through for us, so we create a backup plan just in case. God wants you to come to the place where you so rely on your supply of living water that you *never thirst again*.

Every situation in your life requires a never-thirst-again experience. When my father was in a coma, I had to reach a place where I was no longer trying to find relief, where I wasn't still trying to find my miracle. Something turned after that vision, and I felt satisfied that the miracle was already in manifestation. It was a supernatural moment when I had received my needed drink of living water. Once living water flows over you, you are no longer searching for a drink to relieve the thirst in the situation you are facing. You no longer need to search for answers. There is no fear, and you don't feel anxious anymore.

A never-thirst-again experience is supernatural, because the water is directly from the flow of the Holy Spirit. The Spirit of God is supernatural, and when He moves over you, there is no mistaking His power. To explain this to the woman at the well, Jesus supernaturally demonstrated a never-thirst-again experience. He demonstrated it through the supernatural, because this experience of fulfillment is always supernatural. You can't always describe or even explain it, but you know it's from God.

In verses 16–19, Jesus told the woman to call her husband, knowing she was living with a man outside of marriage. Sheepishly she confessed that she was not married. That is

The Supernatural You

when Jesus demonstrated the supernatural. He said, "You have told the truth. I know you have had five husbands and this is your sixth relationship." Astonished, the woman realized she had met a man of God; she saw the supernatural working right before her very eyes. She immediately recognized Jesus's power and turned her attention toward the mountain she stood upon. Growing up in that region, she knew Jerusalem was the respected place of worship, and she probably expected Jesus to be like other leaders and direct her to it. She was probably surprised that something incredible could take place on the wrong mountain, the one where she was standing. God's power was working right where she was; she didn't have to go anywhere else to find it. She received a never-thirst-again experience right where she was—in her sixth hour.

God's plan is for you to receive your answer, regardless of where you are at the moment. It doesn't have to manifest when the mood is just right or during a praise and worship service. He has shown that He will manifest the power of His Spirit in the least likely location and the most unexpected moment if you will expect His power to work there. All He wants is for you to look inside of yourself at the supply of His wonderful Holy Spirit, which is present on your current "mountain." When you look to your well of supplied living water, you will experience your supernatural never-thirst-again experience, regardless of where you are and what you are going through! God is about to manifest a miracle in your sixth hour!

"I Am Your Exceeding Salary"

A while ago, we were working to expand our ministry both spiritually and physically. As most ministries do, you realize

100

there comes a time when you need to develop a whole new way of operation. What worked last year is not going to work this year. God began to open many doors that confirmed that this was to be our focus. Suddenly, in the middle of our renewed vision, we also realized that the tiniest thing you do costs a lot of money. Everything is expensive! Our printing needed to change. Our methods toward travel needed to change. There was new equipment to buy, and more. It was going to take more people and a new way of thinking. We could no longer have a "ma-and-pop shop" mentality. Suddenly there was more ministry to do than there was money to pay for it.

We did all the things necessary to make it happen, including an expansion of our church building. We acquired an additional 9,000 square feet of building to remodel. The new acquisition also required us to rebuild some of our current space. It was a larger expansion than we had ever undertaken up to that point. We began raising funds and received offerings for the project. God supplied supernaturally, but soon into the project, we recognized that there was going to be more expenses than we anticipated. Many churches find themselves in this situation, and they need the body of believers to stay positive with their support in both faith and finances. One cannot always anticipate the costs that come with the unexpected. We found ourselves in the middle of the unexpected, and God was growing us.

One morning I was praying and talking with the Lord about our next move in the expansion project and about the financial provision to complete it. I knew we were going to need more money, so mentally I was feeling some pressure from it. My prayers were along the normal lines when a person asks the Lord to meet a particular need. I said, "Lord, I thank You that You will provide all we need to pay for this project." I also asked Him to give us the wisdom concerning every plan and step so that we would make all the right decisions. As I came near the end of my praying, I heard the voice of the Holy Spirit speak to me. He said these words loud and clear, "I am your exceeding, abundant salary." Immediately, I recognized those to be the words the Lord spoke to Abram in Genesis 15:1, when He said "Abram, I am thy shield, and thy exceeding great reward." I already knew that verse was talking about wages and salary because in Hebrew that is what the word *reward* means. God offered to him that He would be his source of total abundance.

God was trying to tell me that morning not to worry, that His desire was to take care of every need we had to complete our ministry vision. Do you know that we finished that project with flying colors and every need was met? God supplied all we needed. I believe a part of that was because the Lord gave me that word about provision after I pulled on God's anointing within me. That was what I needed to renew my faith, and, in addition to the many who prayed, it propelled us to supernatural provision for the project.

Then during that same morning of prayer, the Lord also said to me, "I am the complete source of supply for people, and I want to tell them every day how I will supply for them, just as I did for you today." I received the revelation that God was my supply and that He desired to discuss it with me on a regular basis. In fact, it was from that early-morning experience, another never-thirst-again moment, that I developed a page on our Web site (www.ovm.org) called "The Daily Prophecy." I want to help people hear God talk to them every day about their life and circumstances so they can be certain He will take care of them. We all need a daily word from the Holy Spirit! If you listen in your heart, He is in there speaking! He will give you the right word needed to tap into the supernatural power of God. That day, the Lord helped me understand that He is there to speak to your spirit privately. His flow and supply will bubble up from within you and speak to you if you are listening, even when no one else is there to assist you.

After that morning when I heard the Lord speak to me about being my total supply, I further understood the power within. It had to do with my ability to hear His voice. He is in there ever speaking and ever talking. However, the most important thing I discovered was the environment that made His voice come to me so loudly. His voice had come to me in the middle of prayer, but not just any prayer. It was just as I finished praying in the Spirit. From the environment of tongues His voice came. I have found that the more I pray in the Spirit, the more I hear God and the more I experience the supernatural.

Tongues: The Supply of the River

One time as I was getting ready to minister at a meeting in Central America, the Holy Spirit told me to do something different during my preparation time. Normally I study, listen to the Lord for the meeting, and pray both in the Spirit and in English. This time the Lord told me to "preach my meeting in tongues." I knew what He meant by that, so I began to pace the floor and picture the meeting even though I had never actually been to that place. I spent two hours "ministering" to the crowd in other tongues during my private time in the seclusion of my own bedroom. I paced as if I were standing before the hurting and needy in the meeting. The power of God grew as I "preached" in tongues. I disciplined my mind to think only on the meeting.

When I finally arrived at the meeting, God moved in a unique and powerful way. My preaching felt meatier, and people were touched, delivered, and healed. My passion is that people will always leave a meeting with lasting fruit and a permanent change in their life, because I know how it feels to attend a service that changes your life in a very real way.

Afterward in my private prayers, I told the Lord that I was so grateful for the way He touched the people but also for how His Spirit had touched me during the service. The miracles of God had broken forth in a new way after that meeting, because I obeyed the Lord to conduct the meeting in the Spirit first. There was a new flow that came from first forging ground in other tongues. Praying in tongues is like the ground space that is carved out before buildings are built. It is the foundation created before the results. It is the doorway to the supernatural power of God.

I had always prayed in tongues before that, but I had never used it as a "digging" tool to forge ground in front of me quite like that. I began to do that with other meetings and things the Lord wanted me to do, and I saw similar results. I see praying in the Spirit the same way you see visiting some place through virtual reality on the Internet. Through the computer, you can sometimes see and "touch" a place you plan to visit before you actually go there. This is how the Lord intended praying in tongues to work for us. Since praying in tongues is a way that you cause the river from your spiritual well to flow, you can think of it in terms of how rivers have cut through rock and formed places like the Grand Canyon and even the power of Niagara Falls. The water's force went before and created a pathway, a unique and special backdrop that attracts people to it.

Once when my husband was preaching, he told about a

time when he could remember having a great week. Everything seemed to be going fantastic, and he was experiencing many breakthroughs. He took a moment to thank the Lord for that, and he heard the Lord tell him, "Hank, did you notice how much time you've been praying in the Spirit? Did you know that you actually forged the things you are experiencing this week when you did that?" I love that story because it reminds me how much we can be setting things into motion when we pray in the Spirit.

For this reason, we can see why Paul said in 1 Corinthians 14:18, "I thank my God, I speak with tongues more than ye all." He was expressing his appreciation that he had developed a lifestyle of praying in the Spirit. Perhaps it was the reason this apostle wrote most of the New Testament and, according to 2 Corinthians 11:28, he could powerfully oversee most of the early established churches.

It could also have played an important role as to why he knew about overcoming evil spirits. This apostle was the one who confronted the spirit of python in Acts 16:18, which brought the entire city into an uproar. He lived in danger every day in his ministry. He also was in constant confrontation with the religious leaders of the day. Although his reference to tongues in 1 Corinthians 14:18 surrounded its use in the public assembly, he must have found it as a private source of power worth talking about. He would have little need to mention it had it not been a key in his personal life and in his ministerial success for overcoming the powers of darkness. He had a reason to be thankful for it.

Praying in the Spirit is the primary way to cause the river of power to flow from your spirit. That is why it was the *first* manifestation of the Holy Spirit that flowed out of the people in Acts chapter 2. They started in power by praying in other tongues. No wonder the devil tries so hard to keep the church from using it! He has used religious people who will reject it as "gibberish." Others feel it should only be an occasional occurrence. Beyond that, we find Spirit-filled people who have forgotten the power of this flow from the Spirit. They have it but don't use it. Many Spirit-filled believers have treated its emphasis as a "move" of the past and don't pray in the Spirit as they once did. We also have ministers who are fearful that praying in tongues as a group, as they did in Acts 2, might frighten visitors. Fortunately, you just don't find that mind-set in the Bible. As I said before, the Spirit of the Lord wasn't worried about visitors on the Day of Pentecost.

Demon spirits have tried many ways, such as these, to keep the church from praying in tongues, but it is the essential power that opens the flow of the Holy Spirit's anointing. In Acts 8, Simon the sorcerer must have recognized some form of power when the people were filled with the Spirit in Samaria, because he was willing to pay money for it! He wanted to have it himself because he *saw* something (v. 18) had happened. There was some sign that came with the Holy Ghost that he knew to be spiritual power. Realize that this man was a sorcerer. He understood and recognized when he saw spiritual power. Keeping with New Testament consistency of other accounts of those who received the Holy Spirit, I am certain the power he saw was the people praying in tongues. When he saw it, he wanted it so badly that he was willing to pay money to have it. I think there is something terribly wrong when witches will pay for it while Christian people try to hide it. We need a renewed revelation about the power we have through praying in tongues.

DIVERSITY IN TONGUES

At the church my husband and I pastor together, we cultivate an environment for tongues. We encourage prayer in tongues during nearly every corporate prayer meeting. During regular services, we make way for the Holy Spirit to operate in tongues and interpretation, and all our public messages to the people in tongues are interpreted the way the Bible teaches. Occasionally, in a normal service, we have moments of corporate prayer in tongues for special things as the Spirit leads us. However, we have specific settings of prayer just in tongues. There is no public message being given; it is just all the people praying to God in one large room, no differently than how people might all pray and worship together in English. During those times of prayer, we are unrestricted about praying in the Spirit.

As I said earlier, we forge new ground in tongues. We teach people how to endure in that kind of prayer by making some of our prayer meetings a training session for the whole church. We don't just train the intercessors; we train the people. We start with twenty minutes and then stretch to twenty-five and so on. Many groups find it difficult to have corporate prayer in tongues for any length of time because you run the risk of losing some people to distraction or boredom. However, we regularly have extended periods of praying in the Spirit during our prayer meetings to help grow the people beyond that. Now if you ask *our* congregation to pray in the Spirit you had better hold on to your hair! They know how to make the building shake. Maybe that's what happened in Acts 4:31, when the building shook after the disciples and the people prayed. It began to shake as they prayed in tongues, but then shook under the supernatural power of God. We don't know what was the exact case, but we do know that their intense prayer caused something to happen.

Sometimes we have experienced praying in the Spirit when it is so unusual that it almost sounds strange to your own ears. If you didn't have a spiritual sense about you, you might think it odd. However, I have learned to release myself into uncharted territory in the Holy Ghost. The problem is that many people are afraid to step into new waves and new ground for fear of falling into something false. Jesus addresses that problem in Luke 11, when He taught on prayer. In verses 10–13, He assures us that when we are "asking" for the Holy Spirit, or stepping into the Spirit, we can be sure that we will not fall into the wrong thing. Now, that does not mean we cannot make mistakes or miss it sometimes. What it means is that we can trust that when we pray in the Spirit that we will not find ourselves crossing over into a wrong spirit. Wrong spirits are primarily found working in three main environments.

- *Isolation.* False and evil spirits love to isolate you, ministers, and churches where there are no outside supportive relationships or accountability. You can be alone without becoming isolated, but when you develop the attitude that you don't need anyone or that you can't relate to anyone else, you risk getting in a spiritual ditch. The madman of Gadara was isolated when he was bound by demons (Mark 5).

- *False doctrine.* The apostle Peter talked often about those who promoted false doctrine. In fact, the New Testament warns more about false teachers than false prophets. If you are in a church that has right basic doctrine and you are hooked up to believers who are in the flow of God according to the Bible, you will stay accurate in the spirit of prayer both privately and at prayer meetings.

- *Pride.* Whenever the motive is to exalt one's own self or ministry, then eventually the enemy will find a door to enter whether you are operating in the Spirit or just working in the natural. Pride is the main tool of the demonic realm to cause human downfall in every realm. If you want to be seen for your spirituality or great ministry accomplishments and talent, you could end up stepping into areas that will carry a wrong spirit.

If we make the point to stay connected with other Christians through both church and relationships, we keep ourselves from being vulnerable to demons. Then by attending a good church that preaches right doctrine and allowing that anointing to keep you straight, you will find yourself on target in prayer. That doesn't mean we won't make mistakes, but it means overall we will be sound in our approach to spiritual things. Then when we keep ourselves free of pride, we can trust that God will use us accurately in the Spirit.

Be less concerned about getting "off" than you are about getting into the river of the Spirit. This is why so many believers stay on the shore and never enjoy anything fresh from the Holy Ghost. They think there is only one way to do things, and that is the way they have been used to for years. We assume that if we didn't learn it in our "camp," then it is not from God. We become accustomed to one style of prayer, singing, and even preaching, but there are many rivers in God.

My husband preached about a powerful experience he had with the Lord one time. The Lord said to him, "To Moses I was the burning bush, to Joshua the captain of the hosts, and to Ezekiel I was the wheel within the wheel. Who was right?" My husband's answer was, of course, "Lord, they all were!" That is exactly right. They all were right! God manifests Himself in many different ways, and we have to learn to flow with many expressions and trust that if we stay close to Him, we will not get off track. God is a big God, and just because something is unfamiliar to you, that does not mean it is not from heaven. Be open to the Holy Spirit, and He will lead you correctly.

Learn the genuine aspects of the supernatural realm by first forging new ground in tongues. Allow the flow of the Spirit to get deeper in you by practice. I train myself to "turn off" my own ears when I pray in the Spirit. I try to focus less on how loud or quiet I am, and I just let the river flow. Of course, sometimes you are in locations where you can't be too loud, but the key is to let the anointing flow unrestricted. During some of my prayer in tongues, I have heard some wild things come out. Let yourself get lost in it sometimes by turning off what is around you.

The Bible says in 1 Corinthians 12:10 and 28 that there are *divers* kinds of tongues. There are different sounds in tongues, and they don't always come out the same way. I believe these different tongues are the different "rivers" that flow to deal with different things in the Spirit that we need.

We have experienced tongues for nations, unique tongues when praying for America, and other types of tongues when we pray for our city. One time we were praying together during our midweek prayer meeting, and everyone was praying in the Spirit, focusing our prayer toward the nations. There wasn't a large crowd of people, but it was an intense time of prayer. Toward the end, my husband saw a vision of an angel holding a scroll. He read the scroll, and then the angel said to him, "I have come for Israel." We had no idea that we were even praying for Israel; we just were trying to yield ourselves for the nations in general. When the angel entered the room, nearly every person fell on the floor under the power. People stayed there for an unusually long time. When I finally got up, I noticed my arm had been in a still position with my elbow on the ground and my hand raised up. I never even felt it. Normally, I wouldn't be able to do that, but something supernatural happened.

A few days later, Israel was in the news regarding a big event that coincided with the scroll my husband saw. We were shocked. I believe that because of our prayers, the Lord protected what could have been. We have to know that our prayers are powerful when we yield to the Holy Ghost.

During another night of prayer, we were interceding for our city. We prayed in English and asked the Lord to protect it and bless it in general. We asked for God's covenant blessing to come over the city and to protect it. Then we stepped over into other tongues. There was an unusual sound of intercession that night. The musicians were on their instruments and began creating uncommon sounds. Our tongues had many different expressions also. At the close of the meeting, we ended with a glorious time of praise. Then shortly after the service, some of the congregation came running in from outside and told us to come and see something. We went out into the parking lot of our building and looked over the top of the roof and saw a huge double rainbow over our city and church. I believe God was showing us the impact of our prayers through His covenant promise. Something was released from just praying in tongues.

There are things you can release both privately and corporately when you yield yourself to praying in the Spirit. That is where the source of the river flows, just as it did on the Day of Pentecost. There is power in it, and you can rely on it to take you straight to the answer you need from God.

GOD LIKES IT LOUD

We have taught this level of tongues to our church. We've made them pull prayer in other tongues from the depths of their spirit. We wanted them to get into a place where the river could not be crossed over, like in Ezekiel 47. Initially, some of them didn't care for it. They felt more comfortable being the quiet prayer type. Praise God, they stayed with it, and now they are among the most powerful intercessors in our church today. The Bible doesn't really give us personal preferences when it comes to prayer or even praise and worship. There isn't any scripture that teaches us to worship God in our own comfortable style. Instead, it tells us how God likes it done, and the Bible talks more about the use of a loud voice than the use of a quiet one. (See Exodus 19:16, 19; Deuteronomy 27:14; 2 Chronicles 5:13–14; 20:19; 30:27; Ezra 3:12; Nehemiah 9:4; Psalm 29:7–8; 33:3; 46:6; 47:1; 55:17; 66:8; 68:33; 98:4; 149:3, 6; 150:5; Acts 2:2; 4:24; 16:25–26; Revelation 5:11.)

The Lord is not afraid of a loud sound when it is a righteous noise. In fact, if you read enough about Him, you will find out that He is a noisy God! He likes loud instruments and loud singing, and He likes shouting. According to Isaiah 42:10–15, God also likes the sound of a righteous roar. I have concluded one thing: God is not afraid of noise. God likes it loud! Now if you were to go to many churches, you wouldn't see a whole lot of what God likes. The people are very still, very quiet, and the prayer and praise usually never cross a certain level of intensity. Now this doesn't mean everything has to be screaming all of the time, but we have had church so often with more of the quiet things than the things God actually likes. Too many churches, even Spirit-filled ones, are too reserved out of fear that they will not be in order. And yes, of course, there needs to be order, but we have gone so far the other way that we have lost our roar of anointing. I think we need to reverse that and turn up the volume in praise and especially our volume in prayer. In fact, Acts 2:4 of the Amplified Bible indicates that the people actually spoke loudly in tongues on the Day of Pentecost, by describing it with the phrase "as the Spirit kept giving them clear and *loud* expression" (emphasis added).

We tell our congregation that we want to hear them pray with a roar when we all pray in the Spirit together. We put our whole being into prayer both in English and in tongues. It is hard to fall asleep and get bored when you put your body into it! Intensity in prayer that includes your whole being—spirit, soul, and body—will cause your river of anointing to go from a trickle to a flood. When we first started our church, I wanted to be the poised minister's wife who was all put together without a hair out of place. The problem with me is that when I get around the music of the Spirit and when I get around praying people, my river is trained to flood. I can't help it. I have tried to pray quietly, but I can't do it. I get too excited about the Spirit. I have tried not to jump and dance when the anointing is flowing in praise, but it doesn't happen. Finally I quit worrying about that, because I have found that if you will just jump into the roar of the Spirit, you keep weights broken off of you. Strongholds are broken in the atmosphere of loud prayer and praise, particularly if you take part in it. Something happens when you let the river just pull you with its current. You get free—glory to God!

Learn to step into different realms and kinds of tongues. You don't want to pray in the same monotone level of tongues that you did when you were first filled with the Holy Spirit. You need to grow in it the same way you grow as a Christian. Become more mature with it, and follow where the Spirit leads you. I like to say it this way: "Learn to follow the Spirit, and don't make the Spirit follow your preference." Pray in tongues, and let the anointing of it lead you. Don't hold back because it sounds unusual sometimes. That is what it means to step into diversities of tongues. There are different sounds, different utterances and anointings; learn to use all of them. The only way you can grow into it is by practice. You learn it by doing and getting around others who are willing to do the same. The world of other tongues will cause you to flow in the river of your spirit. It will bring the well of anointing out of you to deal with your situation or that for which you are praying.

THE SPIRIT-TO-SPIRIT EXPERIENCE

The woman at the well could not believe what she was hearing and seeing, "How could God move on this mountain and not in Jerusalem?" she thought. "He is telling me my own life's story. He knows everything I have done. He *must* be a prophet, right?" Once the Samaritan woman saw Jesus demonstrate the power of living water, she knew something was different. There was something taking place that had not happened in the region before. Then Jesus began to talk to her about what it was. In John 4:21–24, Jesus said, "Woman, believe me, the hour cometh, when ye shall neither in this mountain, nor yet at Jerusalem, worship the Father. Ye worship ye know not what: we know what we worship: for salvation is of the Jews. But the hour cometh, and now is, when the true worshippers shall worship the Father in spirit and in truth: for the Father seeketh such to worship him. God is a Spirit: and they that worship him must worship him in spirit and in truth."

She probably thought, "He is so unlike the others, saying that God can be worshiped anywhere." The people of that day had been taught that to experience God you had to visit Jerusalem, the location of the holy place that housed the presence of God. Regardless of what she had heard, she knew that she felt the power of God right where she was, and it washed over the hurts in her heart. She couldn't explain it, but Jesus obviously knew her thoughts, so He began to teach her one of the most powerful revelations in the Bible. This was what God looked for with Moses. It was what He wanted from us all along. God wants a Spirit-to-spirit experience with us—His Spirit, the well of supernatural water, connecting with our own spirit.

By giving this revelation to the Samaritan woman first, it was a prophetic message that God's Spirit wants to fill you, no matter who you are or what you have walked through in life. He wants to fill you so that water can be the force of power that will turn everything around.

Jesus used the key phrase in verse 24. He said, "God is a Spirit." That is the answer. God wants to show you *Himself* from within *yourself*! This is where God wants to speak to you and demonstrate His power so you will never feel needy or thirsty in any circumstance. You don't have to be anywhere special to have it. It can be right in your living room or in the car regardless of the situation. Since God is a Spirit, this is what He wants in a relationship. He doesn't want to operate outside of that. That is why God doesn't perform things to prove Himself when people demand it. He knows that His demonstration is not a Spirit-to-spirit relationship. It further helps us understand why Jesus said in Matthew 16:4, "A wicked and adulterous generation seeketh after a sign."

People who always want outward proof first will never enjoy a Spirit-to-spirit relationship with the Lord, and they will feel cut off from God's supernatural power. They will never know how to draw from their well within because they always need to go elsewhere to find an outward manifestation. God manifesting Himself elsewhere is fine, but He *first* wants you to meet Him privately about the issue, and He wants you to experience what His Spirit imparts before something else speaks into it. He wants that river of water to wash over you while it is just one on one. That is what God wants according to John 4:23, and those are the people He seeks to worship Him—people who can look to the One who lives on the inside of them. With that understanding, you will then find that outward manifestations of God will follow.

Immediately she saw it! It must be Him, right? For some sudden reason in John 4:25, this woman at the well brings up the subject of the Messiah. Do you think she said it by accident, or did this Man standing before her know something about the One called Christ? Did she suspect...? Could it be? Well, one thing that is certain is that before Jesus talked about the Spirit-to-spirit experience, she could only think of a random prophet, but afterward she was entertaining that word *Messiah*! I believe God is showing us the revelation that before you experience the Holy Ghost's anointing in the Jacob's well of your spirit, you see things one way, but *afterward* you will see them differently. Your eyes will be opened, and you will have the full revelation of the anointing that stands before you. You will see the Anointed One; you will see the Christ.

No matter what you are facing today, there is a supernatural supply in you that is always available. It doesn't matter where you are, whom you are with, or what impossibilities seem to be looming. It works, and this well of supply will answer everything you need.

Chapter Five

SUPERNATURAL EQUIPMENT IS IN YOUR HOUSE

I T IS WITHOUT question that the anointing of God's power is coming from one unique place, and that is God's house. The real revelation of it doesn't take root until we emphatically realize that *we* are His house. As the entire body of Christ, we are His corporate house. But as an individual, you are also His dwelling place, His house. First Corinthians 3:9 says, "For we are God's fellow workers; you are God's field, you are God's building" (NKJV).

As we explore this, we need to see one very special characteristic the Holy Spirit brought when He filled us. When the Holy Spirit made your spirit His home, according the picture in Ezekiel 47:1, He brought water into the house.

> Afterward he brought me again unto the door of the house; and, behold, waters issued out from under the threshold of the house eastward: for the forefront of the house stood toward the east, and the waters came down from under the right side of the house, at the south side of the altar.
> —EZEKIEL 47:1

It was so much water that you didn't even have to enter the house to see the water. It just came rushing out from under the door. The water of God's Spirit inside us is meant to flow in such a vast quantity that it can't help but spill out. That water contains the tools, equipment, and gifts of the Spirit of God. They are to be so packed in there that they are oozing out of us.

Yet many people are convinced that they are not qualified or spiritually strong enough to have that level of God's Spirit, so they often talk themselves out of it. They simply think their spiritual "equipment" will never be powerful enough in order for them to live as supernatural Christians. Still even more believe that they are never quite "prepared" to flow in the anointing of God for their life or for others. Even many dedicated believers are convinced they can't ever quite measure up. The reason many people struggle with walking in supernatural power is because they feel worthless or condemned about their shortcomings.

One Sunday evening after service, one of our church members came up to me and asked for prayer to be healed. She is a strong woman of God who knows how to stand in faith for God's promises. At the time, I was not fully aware of the potential seriousness of her situation. She began to tell me that she had begun with what seemed like flu or cold symptoms, which then turned to an unexplained severe itching that was maddening. It not only kept her awake at night, but it also made her days miserable.

At first, she thought maybe she was having an allergic reaction or had taken too much pain reliever. However, the symptoms became worse. There was no rash or hives, just a mysterious internal itch that seemed to be under the skin somehow. No creams or ointments could relieve it. The doctors ran routine blood tests that revealed her liver enzymes to be extremely high—three times that of a normal person. The doctor said they had to do more tests, but that initial results were indicating some type of autoimmune disease, which could mean lupus, hepatitis, or liver disease. The problem was that every test they tried never seemed to reveal anything concrete. Doctors just could not conclude what was wrong with her.

She said to me, "I have been praying and speaking the Word of God and also just examining my heart to see if I have opened a door to the enemy in any way that allowed this to come in." When she told me that, I remembered how the Lord dealt with me one time when I was busy condemning myself, feeling like God wasn't answering my prayers because I might have an "open door" I didn't know about.

Do you know how that works? The minute you need God to answer you, the devil is right there condemning you. You find yourself wondering whether or not a sin you committed made you vulnerable to all the attacks you are experiencing. The other scenario is that you are working through repentance and change in an area of your life, but you think God must be disappointed with your progress because the answers to your prayers don't seem to be coming as they should. Of course, we certainly should examine ourselves as the Bible tells us in 1 Corinthians 11:28. Scripture also says in Philippians 2:12 that we must work our salvation out with fear and trembling.

However, there is a vast difference between demonic or self-condemnation and self-examination or conviction from the Holy Spirit. We will touch on this briefly in this chapter, because it keeps many people from using the supernatural equipment God gave them.

First I want to show you something the Lord showed me about answered prayer and our sins. I was able to share it with this woman. It is found when Jesus taught on prayer in Luke 11.

Jesus gave us an example of how to pray. In verse 3, He taught us to ask for our needs, using the example, "Give us day by day our daily bread." Then afterward, in verse 4 He taught us to ask for the forgiveness of sins with the example of "Forgive us our sins." One day the Lord helped me see that it was not by accident that Jesus taught us to ask for our needs *before* we ask forgiveness. This was because the Lord wanted us to know that He is not basing the answers to our prayers on our sins or lack of sins alone.

Yes, we need to strive to live purely as a testimony to Christ in us, and deliberate disobedience will allow the devil to gain access. (See Proverbs 17:19; 28:13; Ephesians 4:27; 1 Peter 5:9.) However, God is not holding out on your answer because of some shortcoming in your life, particularly when you don't have a clue what that might be. Chances are, if you need to repent of it, you already know very well what it is, and the Lord has nudged you many times already to get it corrected. In that case, immediately go to God and get it right, then afterward trust that He wants to answer your prayers.

The devil always wants to condemn you and make you think you have done something bad all of the time, so you never feel confident that you deserve an answer or can access God's supernatural power. Instead, Jesus taught prayer specifically this way so that we would forever be reminded that it is not about our performance of righteousness that will get our miracle. It is about the blood of Jesus and because God is our loving Father, who wants to help us when we reach to Him in faith. Psalm 103:10 says, "He hath not dealt with us after our sins; nor rewarded us according to our iniquities."

I shared this truth with the woman and encouraged her

that she had every right to be healed. I also offered to pray for her. Now I must say that this was one of those days that even though we had just enjoyed a powerful service, I didn't *feel* anything powerful in praying for her, mostly because I was a little tired after the service. So I simply anointed her with oil according to James 5:14–15, which I felt covered her whole situation, just as it does everyone who wants to be healed. It says, "Is any sick among you? let him call for the elders of the church; and let them pray over him, anointing him with oil in the name of the Lord: and the prayer of faith shall save the sick, and the Lord shall raise him up; and *if he have committed sins, they shall be forgiven him*" (emphasis added).

Well, we had all the ingredients, right? We had one pastor (elder), one sick person, some anointing oil, and we were going to pray a faith prayer. I also want to draw your attention to the fact that this verse does not give us any indication that the miracle power will be hindered if the person has sinned. In fact, it says that the person can receive forgiveness along with their healing, and the prayer of faith will work for both.

So in my mind, all of those added together should equal a healing according to this verse. Nevertheless, on that day, I didn't feel a thing when I prayed, and she didn't say she felt anything either. The only thing I felt was a *knowing* she was healed, but I personally didn't feel very anointed in the prayer. There was not a goose bump, my prayer didn't make anything shake, and no lightning came from my hands that I was aware of. I just knew she was healed based on the fact that I know what the Bible says.

The only thing I did feel was that the Holy Spirit was urging me to tell her to drink plenty of water. Seemed like a common thing to say, but I told her anyhow. Again, sometimes the supernatural power is operating in what we think to be ordinary. So after prayer, she left the front of the auditorium. I didn't think too much about it until she sent me an e-mail one day several months later.

She told me that amazingly, one month after we had prayed together, she was given a medication for itching that required her to drink large amounts of water, confirming what the Holy Spirit said. She had also held on to many scriptures that the Lord gave her. She even remembered my husband sharing a testimony about how he was healed one time from a broken arm, that even though he was miraculously healed, the complete process took some time. She felt confident that this was the case with her and that even though she was healed when we prayed, her complete healing was manifesting through a process. She stood for what we prayed that day, deciding not to accept any condemning lie from the devil that would keep her from her healing.

Miraculously, in less than two months time her symptoms had completely vanished! Then two months beyond that her doctors told her that she was totally healed and there was nothing wrong with her. The doctors also canceled all the tests they had previously planned. Her healing was nothing short of a miracle. To me the most amazing part of the miracle was that God manifested His power. It spilled out, even when she and I both felt hampered by our own inadequacies at that moment.

Many Christians and ministers have been faced with situations where they felt inadequate to handle them. It seems like the problem is beyond their level of spiritual skill and anointing or that the problem came at a time when they didn't feel "in tune" to God enough to produce the miraculous. If we were to be honest with ourselves, we have all had those moments. Of course, it always seems like the biggest issues arise during those times. Regardless of how much time you spend in prayer or in the Word of God, some things will still look like a mountain too big to climb. You will feel like you are addressing something for which you are not prepared or have no experience to overcome.

There are three main reasons why we often don't feel confident to produce supernatural results with the power of God in us.

1. Past failures and mistakes. The past can be one of the greatest enemies of the anointing. Your previous experiences are only good teachers if the outcome was favorable to show the power of God. Otherwise, those experiences only serve as a mental note of fear the next time you face the impossible. For example, if you prayed for someone to be healed and they died, you might feel inadequate the next time. Or if you tried to overcome a sin habit and failed several times, you might feel like you cannot ever find victory. Past failures of many people are holding them back from future successes.

2. The problem appears bigger than we are. The other reason many people can't step out and minister in the Spirit or receive a miracle themselves is because they see the size of the mountain. Praying for a hangnail is fine, but they subconsciously feel that healing for blind eyes only belongs to the worldwide healing minister. We feel sure that we can trust God to receive a

harvest in terms of dollars but not in thousands of dollars. If the problem feels too big to you, it is easy to focus on your inadequacies.

3. The problem arises at the most inopportune moments. Sometimes it is not that you don't have confidence in your ability to pray or deal with something. Normally you know that you could rise up in the Spirit and address this type of attack. However, this was not the best day for you! It is when you are just trying to watch a movie or maybe go on a family outing. You aren't feeling geared for a fight with your sword drawn for battle. In many cases, you are just tired and need to regroup. Often problems do come at times when we are lacking in prayer or we don't feel in the game.

The Spirit of God knew that there would be circumstances when, naturally speaking, we would not feel the anointing and any power to overcome. However, from the woman's powerful healing testimony, I realized that it doesn't matter what you feel during a situation; what you feel is not what determines if the anointing in you is working. It works because supernatural equipment is already in you. You are housed with it, and it will work. I certainly didn't *feel* anointed when I prayed for that woman that day, and she was also second-guessing her own confidence, but the power of God spilled out anyway because it was already in our spiritual "houses."

This is what Ezekiel saw in his vision. The anointing was in the house and just rushed out from under the door. The river of God is not based on feeling, even though often you will feel it. The powerful supply within you is based on what you own, the supply of goods you already have. Your job is to sharpen and activate them.

For example, if you are a contractor, you probably have tools that you use to do your work. You don't have to "feel" like you have the tools. You either own them or you don't. In fact, even if you feel tired when you go to work one morning, the tools are still in the back of your truck waiting to be used. They don't leave because you don't feel like using them. You own them; they belong to you. They are available to operate anytime you pick them up and put them to use. Once you plug them in, you don't second-guess if they work.

Philippians 1:19 says, "For I know that this shall turn to my salvation through your prayer, and the supply of the Spirit of Jesus Christ." Paul was saying that his answer was found in two things: (1) Those who prayed for him, and (2) the supply of the Spirit. He was expecting the supply inside him given by the Holy Spirit to be the very thing to relieve him of the trials he was facing. He looked to the equipment he had by the Spirit for his answer. This word *supply* literally speaks of supplies that one might have to sustain all their needs. Those supplies are nourishment, furnishings, equipment, and gifts. In other words, imagine every possible staple, appliance, or other item that might exist in any house that makes it become purposeful and attractive.

The Spirit has given us certain equipment and furnishings inside our spiritual "building" that are there so we can be supplied for or can supply others. God has designed it so that no matter how we feel or what we are facing, there is equipment in us to deal with it. All we have to do is use the equipment. We don't have to work up a special feeling to operate it. It has been provided by the Spirit to work anytime we need it.

CONDEMNATION OR CONVICTION?

We touched earlier on the need to know the difference between demonic or self-condemnation and the Holy Spirit's conviction and learning to examine ourselves properly. Because a lack of understanding in this area often keeps us feeling cut off from the power of God, I think it would be important to examine some differences to help us detect which one is at work in our lives. We want to be liberated to walk in the supernatural. If we live with a sense of condemnation or inadequacy, we won't see the tools God has given us to operate in power. Here are some clear differences between conviction and condemnation:

CONVICTION	CONDEMNATION
Comes to warn you before you sin (John 14:26)	Draws attention and mocks you after you sin (John 8:10–11; Rev. 12:10)
Tells you that you will overcome sin and failure; gives confidence (Rom. 8:1–2)	Makes you fear that you can't overcome your faults; creates uncertainty (2 Tim. 1:7)
Reminds you of God's mercy and forgiveness (1 John 1:9)	Makes you feel unforgiven and always guilty (1 John 3:20–21)
Gives you solutions to overcome (Heb. 13:20–21)	Leaves no solutions or escape (1 Cor. 10:13; John 3:14)

CONVICTION	CONDEMNATION
Gives you the sense of God's fatherly wisdom, discipline, and that He loves you (Heb. 12:5–8)	Makes you feel abandoned by God (Rom. 8:15)
Helps you see a positive future (Jer. 29:11–12)	Makes you only see future defeat so you want to give up (1 Thess. 2:18; Gal. 5:7–8)
Reminds you that you are the righteousness of God in Christ and you don't have to live this way (2 Cor. 5:21)	Tells you that you will never be good enough to be righteous (Rom. 8:34)

When you look at these characteristics, you can easily see how the devil works to keep people feeling beat down. Of course, feeling beat down unjustly by the devil is much different from being someone who lives deliberately in sin, thinking he or she can avoid judgment or consequences (Heb. 10:26). Unfortunately these people are actually placing themselves under Satan's condemning power instead of God's forgiving grace. But for those who have a true desire to serve the Lord and are working to avoid sin in their lives, God does not beat them over the head or make them feel forever guilty of failure. That idea is an enemy of the power of God and will keep you from feeling that you can operate in the supernatural.

GOD IS MAKING YOU

Each one of us is at a different level of growth in our Christianity. If we just make certain every day that we are progressing, we shouldn't feel badly about where we are in our walk today. Let's go back to the verse in 1 Corinthians 3:9, which says, "For we are God's fellow workers; you are God's field, you are God's building" (NKJV). You are the building of God, meaning that He is in the process of constructing you. A lifestyle of holiness and determination to live free of sin is a process.

In fact, Matthew 3:8 says, "Therefore bear fruit in keeping with repentance" (NAS). If you notice, bearing fruit is a process of growth, and it takes time along with consistent nurturing and watering. Everything we do as Christians requires growth and our allowing God to make us. This includes learning to walk in the power of God and developing faith in our ability to do so regardless of our shortcomings, inadequacies, and mistakes. If you allow the Lord to do so, He will build faith in you to walk in the supernatural in spite of these things.

Even though all the equipment to function in the supernatural anointing is inside you, the Lord wants to teach you how to use it with confidence and skill no matter where you are or how you feel at the time.

The "Tag-Team" Anointing

My husband and I do a lot of ministry in tag-team fashion. What I mean by that is in much of our ministry, particularly in our own church, we both keep a microphone nearby and have the mind that at any moment the other one could turn over the platform. When that happens, you have to be ready to step into the anointing already created. Now this is not always easy to do. You are either going to flow high in the river or crash on the shore, especially when there is a very intense prophetic or prayer atmosphere. You can be caught off guard and still have to step up into the anointing. We often minister this way when we lead prayer; we tag-team and have to be prepared to minister in the Spirit without notice.

One night during our midweek prayer service, we were interceding for America and praying that the Lord would intervene in the courts all across the nation. We were all praying in the Spirit, when I stepped into an unusual arena in other tongues. I went over into another realm. The corporate anointing was so heavy that some of the people fell into groaning and travail. The band was playing and prophesying with their instruments with some unusual chords. You could physically feel the weighty atmosphere in the room. Suddenly, I began to call out certain words in English about the court systems and the nation. The birthing got heavier until I was almost unable to handle it, so I walked over to my husband and put the microphone in his hand. He told me later that the weight of the room was so thick that he was almost baffled by it. He said, "For a minute, I didn't know what to do." He just stumbled over the pulpit and before he knew it, he heard himself prophesying about God's purpose for the courts of America stating certain things that would happen that summer. All of it came to pass, and God's purposes were fulfilled.

Then another time when my husband was prophesying over the presidential election quite a few years ago, he became so caught up into the anointing that he just fell out under the power of God right on the stage. There he was out on the floor. I stood near him with my eyes big, because I didn't see that one coming. I didn't know just what to do. I casually stepped over him and went to the pulpit. I just opened my mouth and to my own surprise continued the prophecy. I guess God really is the beginning and the end. My husband gave the beginning and I gave the end!

We have had quite a few of these tag-team stories, but in all of them I have found that I never had time to prepare anything in my mind before my mouth had to be open. I couldn't work up a feeling, try to plan what to say, or anything. We both just had to step up and flow with power without notice. We had to depend on the equipment in us and just flip the switch in our spirit.

If you do the things necessary in private to keep your spiritual equipment in good working order before you need it, then when the time comes, you will be prepared to use it like an expert, even when you don't feel anything extraordinary at that moment. You will find that power will spill out of you. Just as a natural house is cleaned and prepared, your spiritual house needs to be cleaned, prepared, and enhanced on a regular basis so it doesn't become dusty and dry. You want to keep it fresh and overflowing so the tools work on contact.

Preparation for Power

If we want the anointing of God inside of us to flow easily and freely even in the most unexpected situations, we need to prepare ourselves. For example, your natural house may be freshly constructed and remodeled, but if you plan to have guests over, there is usually some preparation necessary so your guests can receive the most benefit from their visit with you. There may be food, accommodations, or décor to be prepared. Typically, you cannot expect to do all the preparations after your guests arrive.

In the same way, we need advance preparation to operate effectively in the anointing. While God has equipped us to house His Spirit, we also need to prepare our "house" to be ready at any moment to manifest the power of God so we can be used to bless those whom God brings into our path.

We also need to be ready to operate in that anointing for our own lives as well. Jesus took the time to prepare His anointing of power. I think the best way to learn how to be prepared yourself to be used in the power of God is to learn from Jesus's example.

In Luke 4:1, we first see that Jesus was full of the Holy Spirit, just as we are filled with the Spirit. Then further down in verse 14, we see that not only was Jesus filled with the Spirit, but He also transitioned into power as He entered into Galilee, now in the power of the Spirit. The infilling of the Holy Spirit is the initial equipment God makes available for us to operate in the supernatural. However, we also need to prepare ourselves for the expert use of that equipment just the way Jesus did so we can function in the supernatural things of God.

There were four key ways that Jesus prepared Himself to manifest the supernatural.

1. Jesus "returned from Jordan" (Luke 4:1).

Jordan is a prophetic example of a life of sanctification and is initially exemplified in water baptism. When Joshua took the lead of the children of Israel after the death of Moses (Josh. 1–3), we find that God instructed him to take the people over Jordan. In Joshua 3:5, Joshua told the people, "Sanctify yourselves: for to morrow the LORD will do wonders among you." Notice how God's genuine supernatural power and holiness were connected.

Then in verse 17 of the same chapter, as well as Joshua 4:1, we see that when the people passed over Jordan, they were referred to as "clean." If we want to operate in the genuine, unadulterated power of God, we need to live clean. We must be dedicated to the call of God in such a way that it drives us to holiness. Jesus returned from Jordan where He was baptized as an example of His dedication to holiness and to His calling.

2. Jesus "was led by the Spirit into the wilderness" (Luke 4:1).

The wilderness is the place where your faith is tested. It is where you learn how to trust God to be your total source and provision. Literally speaking, a wilderness is a place where the resources to sustain life are either limited or nonexistent. You simply cannot rely on the normal things you might have relied on outside the wilderness.

It is important to note, however, that the wilderness is *not* a place of tragic circumstances. Some think because they walk through a tragic event that they are in a spiritual wilderness. But remember, God does not test us through the use of tragedy and evil (James 1:13). Instead, God led the children of Israel into the wilderness to test them and see what was in their hearts (Deut. 8:2). He wanted to see if they would trust Him to provide for their needs even if it meant needing a miracle to accomplish it. However, that season of testing was not God causing or allowing bad or tragic things to happen to them. In fact, when they entered the wilderness everything was just fine! The children of Israel were quite all right; nothing bad was taking place. They were well cared for. It's just that their provision was no longer coming from the resources they had become accustomed to.

Their problems began when they became fearful of this new way of living, which was putting their total trust in the Lord that He would provide supernaturally when the natural resources weren't available. When they didn't see the results they thought they should and in the timing they thought they should occur, they suddenly doubted that God would provide for their needs. They immediately wanted to look for another source to meet their needs rather than trust God's promises.

The wilderness is where you learn to believe God's promises are true even if it looks as if they aren't coming to pass at the moment. In order to confidently manifest supernatural power, Jesus had to place His complete trust in God for everything. He had to learn faith for the supernatural when the natural was saying something else.

3. Jesus "did eat nothing" (Luke 4:2).

This was an obvious point, in that Jesus fasted and prayed. When the disciples of Jesus tried to manifest supernatural power by casting out a demon in Matthew 17:14–21, they couldn't make the power work. When they asked Jesus why, He said two things: first, that it was because of their unbelief, and second, that this kind of evil spirit goes out by prayer and fasting. Jesus wasn't saying that every time you meet up with this kind of demon you need to put the deliverance session on hold until you go out and fast and pray first. He was saying that by making a habit of prayer and fasting, you position yourself to walk in the kind of faith needed for this type of miracle manifestation. Jesus fasted and prayed to prepare Himself for the supernatural anointing.

4. Jesus was "forty days tempted of the devil" (Luke 4:2).

Jesus also had to prevail in personal spiritual warfare. He had to learn to overcome temptation. Part of the learning process of walking in the power of God is using that power to destroy your own personal strongholds and temptations toward evil. Jesus was not just tempted only to do the three things the devil tempted Him with in Luke 4. He was actually in direct warfare with the devil for forty full days. Hebrews 4:15 says Jesus was tempted in *all points* as we are, yet without sin. Note that these were real temptations to Jesus, not just situations that somehow had no impact on His thoughts. However, I believe the three temptations specifically listed here reveal three main temptations every one of us must overcome in order to increase God's miracle power in our lives.

Jesus overcame the comfort of His flesh.

In Luke 4:3–4, the devil tempted Him with food knowing He was already extremely hungry. Well, of course, there is nothing wrong with being hungry and wanting to eat after forty days of fasting. So what was the devil after? Satan wanted Jesus to use the supernatural anointing in Him for His own gain—for self-gratification. Now you can certainly call on the anointing of God in you to meet your personal needs, but what we cannot do is use it to meet those needs for selfish purposes that take our focus off the Lord.

Notice Jesus responded by saying, "Man shall not live by bread alone, but by every word of God" (v. 4). In other words, He was saying, "I am not going to take My focus off God's Word so I can get what I want; God's Word comes before my wants, needs, and desires." Jesus could have easily given in to His flesh that was crying out to be satisfied. Unlike Esau who gave in to his flesh for a bowl of soup (Gen. 25:29–34), Jesus wouldn't give away His inheritance of God for self-gratification.

Jesus overcame pride.

In Luke 4:5–8, the devil showed Jesus all the kingdoms of the world and their glory. Satan offered them to Jesus if He would worship him. Now we know the earth and all its fullness is the Lord's. But the worldly systems of this age are governed by the devil; the Bible calls him the "god of this world" (2 Cor. 4:4). Many people today have sold out or "worshiped" the god of this world in order to enjoy what the kingdoms of this world have to offer. The devil is happy to give you a platform if you will take your worship away from God and exchange it for pride and self-worship.

He also wanted Jesus to give in to the pride of being credited for being the king over the world's systems. We know Jesus is the King, but at that time He was not going to be credited for that. He came to die, not set up an earthly kingdom. Jesus countered that temptation by placing the focus of worship back on the Lord.

Jesus refused the kind of fear that wants God to prove Himself.

We see this in Luke 4:9–12, when the devil wants Jesus to throw Himself off the temple just to see if God would save Him. Jesus didn't have to make God prove His presence by doing this miracle. Asking God to prove if He is really there by showing a sign or doing miracles is tempting the Lord. This was how the children of Israel tempted God in the wilderness. They kept saying, "Is the LORD among us, or not?" (Exod. 17:7). Of course, God couldn't seem to display enough signs and wonders to convince them. They just kept on questioning if God was still around.

You see, no matter how many times God does miracles, if you already don't trust He is always with you no matter what, you won't trust even when the supernatural power is at work right before your eyes. Why do you suppose the power worked so powerfully with the three Hebrew boys in the Book of Daniel? They were saved from the fiery furnace in a miraculous way, but notice what they first said. Paraphrasing their words in Daniel 3:17–18, they told the king, "Listen, king, our God is able to deliver us from you without a problem, but even if He doesn't, we won't bow down." They didn't need to see a miracle to be confident in the Lord's power or His presence. As a result, they saw the supernatural power save them from an impossible situation.

We can see that after Jesus made the right preparations, He was ready to manifest supernatural power from the anointing He carried. Luke 4:14 says, "And Jesus returned in the power of the Spirit into Galilee: and there went out a fame of him through all the region round about." Jesus came out of the wilderness ready to walk in the anointing for miracles. And this is what God wants for His body of believers.

A SKYSCRAPER IS RISING UP!

Prophetically speaking, the Lord is preparing the body of Christ to house the presence of His Spirit in a way that will become very prevalent to the world. God wants it to be unmistakable. One of the reasons the Lord was so angry over the tower of Babel (Gen. 11) was because it represented a unified building, inhabited by people of one language and purpose. In Genesis 11:6, the Lord said about the tower, "And now nothing will be restrained from them, which they have imagined to do." They were building a counterfeit, polluted image of what God prophetically planned for the church.

Notice when they were building the tower of Babel, they planned it to become an amazing skyscraper. They intended for it to reach to heaven. Now that didn't start because someone just came up with a fun idea one day. It was a direct assault on Almighty God and His plan for a building of people called the church. We are God's "skyscraper in the Spirit." This is exactly what God had planned for people before the world began. He wanted a building of people to inhabit, one that would have one heart and one language. That is another reason the devil hates praying in tongues! It represents the restoration of a unified language that supersedes natural limits. In the power of the Spirit, we are of one heart and one language.

You can expect to see that God will be very dedicated about displaying His building, the church. In fact, the Bible says we are a city set on a hill that cannot be hid (Matt. 5:14). You can hide small buildings, but skyscrapers are easy to spot, and they are intricately designed. They are usually furnished with the best equipment and most modern conveniences. People are also very attracted to them. Think about how excited you feel when the skyline of a city you are traveling toward comes into view.

People like tall buildings. God is not just building us, but you could say He is making us spiritual skyscrapers. We will be easy to see, and the world is either going to be attracted to our power or despise us because of it. In the past, many have seen the church like empty, deserted property that is always defeated, struggling to make it and without any power. They have seen us like a small building with no electricity or furniture. That was never God's design for the church. The world is about to see a building of people fully furnished with some powerful equipment that we have come to use.

As a result, we are going to come into a season where we will fulfill a prophetic purpose that will defy what the devil once tried to create with the tower of Babel. Similar to what God said about Babel, I am convinced nothing will be restrained from us that we purpose to do in the power of the Holy Spirit. Many will find a place of shelter and fulfillment that God's incredible building will provide. Inside they will find the presence of the living Christ. As we fulfill that purpose, we will reach places in the Holy Spirit that are without limit.

As God's building, He didn't leave us empty. Through the infilling of the Holy Spirit we are fully equipped, fully furnished, and fully supplied. The equipment to flow in supernatural power is ready and available for use. For example, I don't have to walk through my house every day wondering if the couch is there. No, it is already in there and available. I don't have to feel it first to know it is true. Not once have I stopped to determine whether or not I can sit on it because I am not sure it exists. I also don't even have to feel worthy enough before I sit on it.

In the same way, you don't have to question if the spiritual furnishings inside you exist either. God sees you fully furnished by the power of His Spirit. You can be confident that power of the Spirit is there ready to be operated and be utilized, but even more powerful is that it will often work even when you don't realize it. It spills out of the house (Ezek. 47).

Back when we first started our church, a lady visited one Sunday morning. She didn't look particularly normal either. There was something odd about her, but she came in and just sat down in the back. She was an older, heavier woman wearing a dark blue flowered dress. I had just come out and walked onto the stage when the service started, but my husband hadn't walked out yet. The musicians took their instruments and counted the start to the first song. At that exact moment, I looked out over the congregation and just saw some blue flowered material waving around in the back. I wasn't sure what was happening until the ushers all rushed over and I realized it was this woman. The very minute the music started, she had manifested a devil. All I could see was her blue flowered dress waving around.

Our church was still new, and we were trying so hard to

keep it feeling orderly, but all I and the rest of the people on the stage could see was this woman in a blue flowered dress flapping up and down out of control. She began screaming and wetting the floor as the ushers removed her from the room. It was quite a scene! My husband met the ushers in the hall and cast the devil out of her. He dealt with the demon while several men had to hold her down, and then afterward she ran out of the building.

Now the incredible thing is that we didn't do anything to stir up her demon except start the service. The anointing we carried stirred something without anyone realizing it. The power of God just automatically spilled out and caused a demon to manifest because he felt threatened.

Many Christians have had this happen; when they come into close proximity with someone bound by devils, the demons start to manifest. You don't even try to do anything to stir them up. You can just be minding your own business, walking through the shopping mall, and someone starts to scream and growl at you. It is because you are fully furnished, and the supernatural equipment in you from the Holy Ghost will stir up demons and do miracles when you aren't even trying to minister in the anointing. You are God's fully equipped building and adequate to operate what is inside it, and the Lord is creating you with powerful "skyscraper" proportions.

This is exactly what happened with Jesus. A woman was healed just by touching the hem of His garment when He wasn't looking (Mark 5:25–34). The anointing moved, and Jesus didn't feel it until after it happened. The same thing happened with the apostle Peter. People were trying to touch Peter's shadow to get a miracle (Acts 5:15). The power inside of him began operating automatically before he even knew it.

While he was busy ministering to the people in front of him, the ones behind him in his shadow got delivered and healed too. Because Peter knew what he carried, his spiritual equipment began to operate on its own. The water overflowed!

THE REMODELED HOUSE

When you were saved and born again, God completely remodeled you. According to 2 Corinthians 5:17, once you came into Christ you were rebuilt. The old structure was taken away, and everything has been re-created. It is like a spiritual remodeling project. That is why I can't understand why people feel that constantly reliving their past and trying to understand it will be the answer to fix the future. No, I believe that God wants to permanently erase the evils of your past so much so that your mind is renewed in such a way that it will be as if the memory of it was about someone else. The old mental footprints are filled in with a new way of thinking and memories. The old man is destroyed, and the new man is there to be furnished and decorated.

The problem is that many people want to go back to the house before it was rebuilt, because the process of remodeling takes some sacrificial decisions. If you have ever been through a remodeling project, you will know that there is nothing fun about the process. The only good thing is the result when the work is over. Before that time, you are inconvenienced by construction materials, messes, and dust everywhere. Sometimes you even have to move to a temporary location. Many people who have remodeled a kitchen find themselves eating TV dinners and take-out meals for weeks.

In the Spirit, when God remodeled you through the construction material called the blood of Jesus, it was a dramatic moment and a process all at once. The new construction obligated you to leave your present place. This is where many people who fear the change process return to the world. Relationships and lifestyle habits have to be adjusted, and in some cases one may have to find a new occupation. The God-ordained remodeling process causes everything to change.

The process of remodeling is not always enjoyable or convenient, but the end result is always well worth the effort. Nothing can compare to the feeling of entering a room with fresh paint and new carpet, floors, and other finishing work. The smell is different, and you hardly recall how it used to look. This is what God did for you when you were saved. Before He installed all the interior features of the Holy Ghost inside of you, He rebuilt you and remodeled you. This way you would be brand-new and able to house the glory and river of the Spirit even at a flood stage, when virtue begins to spill out involuntarily. God has already enabled you to handle the anointing in all the many ways it flows from your "house."

THE "SOUP BOWL" PROPHECY

One way that the supernatural anointing can "spill out" automatically, so to speak, is through spiritual dreams and even visions. Dreams are part of your supernatural equipment too (Acts 2:17). You don't try to make them happen, they just do. Of course, doing the necessary things to create an environment for the supernatural that we have already talked about in this book will promote the occurrence of spiritual dreams and visions.

One time I had a dream about someone I know. Later in a service where I was ministering, I saw him and prophesied to him about the dream. I told him that I saw him sitting at a dinner table where the server kept trying to feed him a particular bowl of soup. In the soup were all sorts of evil and inedible things. Each time the soup came to his table, he picked up a spoon to eat the soup. Finally, after being served several times he decided he hated the soup and became angry about it and yelled, "I didn't order this, and I don't want it!" On the server's last attempt to bring him the soup, the man took his spoon and slammed it down to the table. As the spoon came down, his hand hit the side of the bowl, flipping the bowl of soup over onto the floor. He was so happy. He stood up to the evil soup and the one who kept serving it. He realized that he didn't have to "eat" what the devil and life had been serving him. He didn't have to receive the devil's "soup" that he had for so long accepted from his past as the normal way of life.

The virtue of the Holy Spirit just spilled over and gave him what he needed from the Lord. It operated even when I didn't have to work it up or feel spiritual. The equipment in you is ready to work all the time.

THE EQUIPPED HOUSE

The wonderful thing about God is that when He remodels us, He doesn't leave us with an empty house. Many believers act as if they are living in a brand-new but empty house. As much as anyone could enjoy a new home, it would wear off fast if you had to live in it without furniture. Acting as if we're powerless and unable to pull the supernatural blessings of God from within our own spiritual house is the same as living in a new but empty construction.

God is an incredible master builder and makes certain that when construction comes to a close you are equipped with the best spiritual technology. Every switch, special lighting feature, and appliance is carefully placed to accomplish different but specific tasks. This is the full supply of equipment you received when you were baptized with the Holy Spirit. The tools and equipment of the Holy Spirit are also known as His gifts. Found in 1 Corinthians 12:8–10, the gifts of the Spirit are the tools of power. They equip your "remodeled house" to function with spiritual electricity. These gifts of anointing are what make the house come alive and be useful.

The gifts of the Spirit can be used for other people, but they are also useful for you. Most people never even think to operate in the gifts of the Holy Spirit for themselves. Why not? Yes, you can prophesy to yourself. If most people would start doing so, they would have a lot of breakthroughs.

We need that kind of power for ourselves. Without it, it would be like a house with no electricity. A house without power will eventually feel like nothing more than a shed and begin to get uncomfortable. The temperature wouldn't be right. You would have no way to cook anything or even turn on a light. Without power, the house would potentially become a breeding ground for bacteria and mold. In our lives, without the regular flow of the Holy Spirit's power and operation of the gifts of the Spirit, our atmosphere will become uncomfortable and out of balance. We won't be able to produce anything. We need the function of power to keep contaminants and bacteria of the world from growing. It is difficult to keep the place pure and clean without any power. Power will regulate the house. Supernatural power working from within you will also keep your spiritual house working right.

This is the supply of power from the Holy Spirit Paul referred to in Philippians 1:19, and it was the source he depended on to overcome trials and to empower his ministry. The way to keep your power fresh and connected to the source is by regular prayer and fellowship with the Holy Spirit, then step out and use what is in you.

THE FURNISHED HOUSE

Of course, if having a newly constructed home were not enough and then for it to be equipped with state-of-the-art power, God made you and me to house the finest spiritual furnishings available. However, the only way we can shop for them is by browsing and "purchasing" from the store of the Spirit called the Word of God. Second Timothy 3:16–17 says, "All scripture is given by inspiration of God, and is profitable for doctrine, for reproof, for correction, for instruction in righteousness: that the man of God may be perfect, thoroughly *furnished* unto all good works" (emphasis added).

A well-furnished home is what makes it complete. It creates an environment that attracts people and comforts them. The Word of God working and developing character and skill in your Christianity is what will attract people and cause you to enjoy life. Having a spiritual house furnished by the Word of God is something you do your whole life.

Think about it; buying furnishings for your house is a process you will probably continue for many years. Just about the time you think you have well furnished every room, something begins to look dated, and it's time to "refresh" the décor. It is the same with Scripture working in your spiritual house. You have to continually update the "rooms" in the Spirit. Just about the time you think you know everything there is about divine healing, the fruit of the Spirit, or the tithe, you will find you have to refresh those things. While you are busy decorating other important rooms, such as developing the prophetic, prosperity, and evangelism, you will realize that some other rooms you worked on years ago have become "dated" again and need to be redone. It takes a lifetime of impartation, study, review, and refreshed revelation to keep your spiritual décor up to date with the Holy Spirit. That is because He loves fine furnishings in the Spirit and wants them fresh and functional all the time.

The Working House

As God's spiritual buildings, we can have all the power of the Holy Ghost and all the character of God and anointing within, but if we don't have a place for that power and good to work, then we will eventually find ourselves dusty relics of the past.

Many believers today are relics of the past because they never got into position for their "house" to work. There is no outlet for their anointing. Every spiritual house needs a place to be used by God so it can be a supply to someone else. Ephesians 4:16 says it plainly: "From whom the *whole* body fitly joined together and compacted by that which *every joint supplieth*, according to the effectual *working* in the measure of every part, maketh increase of the body unto the edifying of itself in love" (emphasis added). In other words, every individual "house" of the Holy Ghost needs to work and supply the larger corporate "house" called the body of Christ. Here are three main ways to get your spiritual house working so it is useful.

1. Find a good local church.

A local on-fire church will give you a plug into a power outlet in the kingdom of God. Your gifts (equipment) and furnishings (talents) will find a place to be used among the consistent environment of a church family. Never accept the lie that you don't need a pastor or church. Of course, there is no perfect church, but you still need a spiritual family to let your purpose develop. Get connected, involved, and place your tithe there. Your money and heart will go together. Your spiritual house is much more vulnerable and meaningless all alone without a consistent family to dwell with. A family will help find leaks in your roof and help you do repairs when you need them. Determination to stay in a local church will also force you to work with other people in love and avoid a critical spirit.

2. Use every room in your spiritual house regularly.

Some people just want to focus on one thing or another when it comes to spiritual things. Some are all the way on healing, while others are apostolic only. Beyond that, some are groups focused only on missions or something else. The truth is that we need all of these.

If your church or present situation doesn't provide an easy outlet for you to pray for the sick, make certain first that you are using the rooms you can. If we are not careful, we can become frustrated and critical until we lock our spiritual front door and find ourselves using nothing. We can easily get so caught up in our favorite, main "living room" that we let other important rooms of the Spirit get stale and dusty. Allow God to open a place for you to grow in the area you are specifically called to by first assuring that you are using the rooms that are most useful for your current spiritual climate.

If you are in a church that is primarily evangelism oriented and you can't find a church that is prophetic, then use the furnishings that will work in that setting. Sometimes we try so hard to grow "palm trees" in the "northern woods," so to speak. Use the furnishings from your other spiritual rooms that work where you are right now. It will keep your spiritual house functioning properly until God brings you into the right setting you need.

3. Find an unlikely place to use your spiritual equipment.

While some people can't seem to stay consistent in a church, there is a whole other group of people who won't leave the pew. They think Sunday is the only time they can prophesy or cast out demons. Too many make the mistake of thinking that our spiritual house can only work and find a purpose in the local church. However, in addition to that environment, the early church also took the furnishings and equipment of their anointing to the most unlikely places. They took them out into the world with those who had never experienced the power of God.

The "Drive-Through" Prophecy

You can be anywhere and trust that virtue will flow out of you from the equipment within the river of your spirit. Once after we had finished ministering at a meeting, we were on our way to the airport. My husband told our driver that before we left, we would pray for him and his wife. In all the busy schedule of the meeting we almost forgot, until it came down to the last day. The only time left was on our ride to the airport. We felt a little bad that we had forgotten and felt like the ride to the terminal seemed like we "crammed in" the prayer, but it was all we could do, so we prayed anyway.

So there we were cruising down the freeway, intending to give a brief prayer, but suddenly God began to minister to this man and his wife. It felt like "drive-through" ministry, real quick and to the point. My husband prophesied that they would give birth to a baby girl, which they had been praying about. I told them that the Lord was going to "cut through some red tape" with some legalities for which they were trying to find closure. We said amen and jumped out at the airport. It felt rushed, but God brought these "drive-through" prophecies to pass in their lives! Rushed or not, it was wonderful to them and just what they needed to hear. More than ever, I was convinced that spiritual equipment operates when we place the demand on it because it is already in the house. Even when we were in a hurry and didn't feel as focused as we might have been otherwise, the river flowed beautifully.

That is why you can trust the river in your house to work for your own life also. I knew a lady who was planning to buy a new car. She shopped around and found one, but after taking it from the lot, she just didn't feel peace or even thrilled about her choice. She kind of hinted with the dealer about returning the car, but their response was that the sale was final. However, she just kept feeling God wanted her to have something better. I believe that the Holy Spirit was nudging her and letting her know that this was not her car. You see, there was supernatural equipment in her that was there to be a blessing.

Thankfully, she followed the sensing of the Spirit and decided that this was not her car. She could have just said, "Oh well, the dealer said I can't bring the car back, so I guess I am stuck with it." Instead she went with what she felt from the Lord even though it didn't look realistic or feel possible. She located a car at another dealership and even proceeded to fill out the paperwork. She declared in prayer that the first dealer would take back the first car. My husband also prayed with her, and they declared that she would get her heart's desire. Within two hours time the general manager who had told her the sale was final called her and said, "Go ahead and bring back the car if you want; we will cancel the transaction!" I believe that was because she chose to use the equipment of the Spirit inside of her, it produced supernatural results.

You don't have to be concerned that you are lacking in your ability to produce the miraculous. Some simply walk more often in the supernatural because they have practiced drawing from the well inside them and refuse to let their own shortcomings hinder them. They make a point to pull from it on a regular basis. The greatest way to use the equipment God has given you is by using it for yourself. Many churches often try to teach people how to pray for the sick and how to prophesy, and there is nothing wrong with that. What we don't often teach people is how to utilize those same tools of the Holy Spirit for their own personal needs. This is where most people are far less confident. Whether for your needs or to minister to someone else, the equipment of the Spirit is available in the river of your spirit to use all the time.

LIVE FROM YOUR POWERHOUSE

In the tabernacle of the Old Testament, the presence of God was "housed" inside a special box known as the ark of the covenant. It was a special box covered in gold with two angels over the top of it. It was then set up in a special place in the tabernacle called the holy of holies. This was the room allowed to be accessed only by the high priest, the room where he went to offer sacrifice for the sins of the people.

It is essential to know that the ark of the covenant was merely a natural model of what God wanted us to become. He never wanted to live in a natural box; He always wanted to live in us. He wanted us to be His holy dwelling. Now inhabited by the Holy Spirit, we carry in our "ark" the spiritual fulfillment of what was inside that Old Testament golden box. The ark carried the physical representation of what we carry in our spirit right inside our own being. It is meant for you to depend on for everything you could possibly need in your life. God has made you to be nothing less than a powerhouse of His Spirit, exploding with all the rich resources of heaven.

Hebrews 9:4 says that there were three items placed inside the ark. They were the rod of Aaron that grew almonds (Num. 17:8), one golden pot of manna, and the tables of Moses, or the covenant. You carry in your spiritual ark the following similar attributes:

1. Supernatural results. Aaron's rod that bloomed supernaturally is your authority that produces miracles. A rod always speaks of authority and position. For us it is the power and authority of God that we carry that will always yield miraculous results.

2. Inheritance of blessing. The golden pot of manna is our rich inheritance as Christ's body. Manna represented Jesus, the Word of God. We are His body seated inside His rich inheritance. In that inheritance are God's natural and spiritual gifts, furnishings, equipment, tools, and resources. We can enjoy all the benefits of the household.

3. Eternal loyalty. The tables of the covenant are the contract we have with God forever sealed by the blood of Jesus. It is an eternal commitment by God to us that we should reciprocate. It means that all God's promises are sure, and our commit-

ment to believe and follow all of them will cause
us to live in peace and safety.

Each of these is carried in the "ark" of our spirit, making
us a powerhouse of the Lord. They flow out through the river
of the Holy Spirit Himself and touch the situation we are
facing. If we cultivate from all three of the categories in our
spiritual ark, we will begin living as the powerhouses God
intended.

Here are some ways that you can begin living from your
powerhouse of supernatural equipment:

1. Expect the supernatural.
2. Speak and find the blessing of God in every
   situation.
3. Use what God gave you.
4. Trust God's promises.
5. Be loyal to God in prayer, obedience, and love.

If you will begin with these simple principles and learn to
practice them until they become a natural response for you,
then it will become easy to live from a powerhouse position
instead of a defeated one. That is what living from the well of
the Spirit is all about. It is taking what God has deposited in
you, pulling from it, and making it your resource for living.
This is what we have been made for; it is in our DNA.

We are God's spiritual building, fully equipped, supplied,
and furnished. There is no limit to what we can accomplish
through His power. You might feel inadequate to address
certain things, or maybe you are facing a problem that
feels too big to handle, but we all have the same power and
equipment in our spiritual house. The secret to living in it

is a lifestyle of practice. Every time you are faced with a decision, ministry opportunity, temptation, trial, or attack, learn to pull from the river of equipment inside you. Once you experience victory and success that way, it will be hard to go back to anything else. It isn't about feeling it as much as it is about using it. You have the ability to use what is in your spirit because God's supernatural equipment is already in your house.

Chapter Six

DON'T JUMP OUT OF THE RIVER

O F ALL THE people in the Bible who probably had the hardest time trying to learn what it means to walk after the Spirit, Peter was the one who stands out. During the years while he followed Jesus on Earth, he would fly into things full swing, and then you would later find him frustrated. One of his greatest endeavors of faith is when he walked on the water to Jesus. Many people have applauded his attempt for even getting out of the boat, but Jesus didn't feel that way about it. In fact, the Lord rebuked him for his unbelief by saying, "O thou of little faith." The Lord wanted him to stay *on* the water. This story gives us an awesome picture of how we can be so easily tempted to jump out of our river of the Spirit once we have tried to step into it. Matthew 14:28–32 says:

> And Peter answered him and said, Lord, if it be thou, bid me come unto thee on the water. And he said, Come. And when Peter was come down out of the ship, he walked on the water, to go to Jesus. But when he saw the wind boisterous, he was afraid; and beginning to sink, he cried, saying, Lord, save me. And immediately Jesus stretched forth his hand, and caught him, and said unto him, O thou of little faith,

wherefore didst thou doubt? And when they were
come into the ship, the wind ceased.

Peter had every intention of accomplishing an incredible
feat, but there were several extenuating circumstances that
he didn't account for. He wanted to walk out onto the water,
but after he stepped out, he became unsure of his own ability
to stand. He believed Jesus could do it, but he didn't feel as
confident in his own power after he tried it, so he wanted to
go back where it felt safer. In the last chapter, we talked about
how people feel inadequate, so they never try to flow in the
supernatural. Here I want to focus on how many people get
started tapping into the anointing but after a time give up,
quit, or get distracted. Like Peter, we see the situation, we
remember past failures, and we jump back out of the water
and go back to what was familiar. Then we look to someone
else who can save us, just as Peter did with Jesus.

Again, let me reiterate that there is nothing wrong with
getting help from someone else, because we need each other,
but the Lord wants you to learn first how to trust your ability
to walk in your own anointing, not just for a short time but
also for the long haul. Most confidence is developed through
consistency and years of determination. The Lord wanted
Peter to have confidence that he could stand and keep
standing.

Verse 29 says that Peter actually did walk on the water.
He actually produced a visibly supernatural occurrence. So
what made him stop? It's possible that Peter didn't really see
what he did. Instead of seeing that he was succeeding, he saw
circumstances that told him he was failing.

Isn't that also what we do sometimes? We receive powerful
answers to our prayers, but when a storm starts to blow our
way, we forget the times we actually walked on the water.

We forget how many miraculous things we pulled right from the well of our very own spirit. I believe this is what Jesus was trying to show the disciples. He wanted them to develop confidence so they wouldn't quit in tough times. Even though they hadn't yet been filled with the Spirit, the day was coming when they were going to have to let the supply of the Holy Spirit be their supporting foundation as they ministered the gospel and performed miracles. They couldn't just jump out of the river when they were confronted with resistance. This is what the Lord wants for you and me today; He wants us to feel completely confident that the river of the Spirit inside of us is a safe place to stand and we don't have to jump back in the boat because it's getting a little windy out there!

From Peter's experience of walking on water, we will see what hindered him from staying with it and discuss that throughout the remainder of this chapter. Often we get tempted, distracted, or discouraged by some form of persecution or problem, so we jump out of the water. This is why many churches, even Spirit-filled ones, have begun to come away from the manifestations of the supernatural and no longer make a place for it in their services.

Jesus's walking on the water is a prophetic example that water is a stable place to stand. In other words, you can rely on the water of the Spirit that lives in you more than anything else, which is so opposite of how many Christians live. Jesus's walking on water was to reveal that it was a dependable foundation of support. Peter jumped out of the water because he didn't think it was going to support him amidst the circumstances all around him. He needed a backup plan. That is the reason, I believe, Jesus was so tough on him and corrected him for having little faith. The Lord wants us to have faith that the anointing the Holy Spirit gives to us is dependable, and we can feel safe that it will support us in every situation. Satan and his demons create all sorts of challenges to make us want to run screaming from the water as if it were infested with sharks! Let's follow a journey to reveal every mysteriously hidden trap the devil has planted to chase us out of the river of the Holy Spirit that we possess.

INTO UNCHARTED TERRITORY

When we first began in the ministry nearly twenty years ago, we thought we were armed and ready for the battle. We knew what we were called to do, and I mean we were moving on to do it. We had received confirmations and prophecies, and our hearts burned for the call. In our minds, we had completely mapped out our future. Everyone is supposed to have a vision, right? If you are in the ministry, you are supposed to know what you're called to do, when you will do it, *and…*who is going to help you pull it off. At least, that is what those pursuing ministry want everyone to think! Suddenly we realized that our carefully prepared lifelong map to ministry didn't reveal that there were some rocky, uncharted wildernesses. We didn't know that we would wake up one morning and have no way to pay our rent and no place to preach. That part was not in the prophecy!

We didn't know it yet, but the Holy Ghost was leading us into uncharted territory on purpose. There was some rough ground that our map didn't show. We were all prepared to take our powerful anointing to the world, but like Peter, we didn't expect it to be so windy when we got out of the boat. One day I remember feeling that we had a real breakthrough because I had thirty dollars left over after paying the bills to buy some food and toiletries. To me, that was a prosperous week. We went on like this for almost one year.

For many people, a situation like this is all it takes to cause them to jump out of the river of the Spirit. They feel like nothing is working and they are failing. They start to think their prayers are not being answered. When we didn't have a dime to our name, we kept praying, prophesying, and using our spiritual equipment to fight our way into the call of God. We kept pursuing it, even when it didn't look like anything supernatural was happening. We would pray in the Spirit, and things got worse. We prophesied, and nothing changed. It seemed like we weren't anointed for it. This is the first trap that the devil uses to convince most people to run back to shore. You didn't expect the wind, so you quit walking on the water and quit believing in the anointing inside of you. Then all of a sudden, one day things began to change for us, and the blessing of God began to unfold on every side. Because we kept pouring forth supernatural power, we eventually saw breakthrough. The Lord was teaching us how to walk through challenges and come out of it still confident that we were anointed.

Jesus wanted Peter to walk through the unexpected and still know with full confidence that he was anointed. Everyone who wants to manifest miracle power must learn this lesson. Instead of doubting what is in the well of our spirit, we need to have confidence in it even when we are walking through the expected. The outward situation is not the determining factor as to whether or not the power of God is working through you. Just because the doctor gave you a bad report today does not mean the things you prayed and spoke into the realm of the Spirit yesterday didn't work. Feel confident that you have the necessary weapons to overcome any potential predator that was not foreseen on your map. The equipment of the Holy Spirit will work while you are traveling through uncharted ground. The wind can still be blowing even while you are successfully walking on water. You can be successfully drawing from your well of spiritual supply while the wind around is boisterous. That is why we can't measure our failure or success to operate the anointing by the outward appearance of things.

God deliberately led the children of Israel by way of the uncharted wilderness on their way to the Promised Land. The Lord gave them numerous reasons to trust that His power and guidance were among them. He parted the Red Sea, brought supernatural water from a rock, rained manna from heaven, and even guided them by a heavenly cloud. Even with all that power working, they still couldn't trust that the Lord would do miracles to bring them through the unexpected. They took the unexpected as a failure of the power of God. Learn to trust that the well of your own spirit will work powerfully in uncharted territory. Often like the children of Israel, the miraculous things of God are very visible, but we don't believe it because we don't have the confidence that our own anointing could accomplish it and that it is working in spite of us being in unchartered territory.

WE HAVE NOT GONE THIS WAY BEFORE

When Israel finally came to Jordan, after Moses had died, Joshua prepared them for the next place they were about to go. In Joshua 3:1–6, the Israelites came to the river, and he instructed the people to position themselves carefully so they could easily see the ark of the covenant moving in front of them. Then when they saw it, they were to follow the direction of the ark. Remember how we talked about our spirit being the house, or "ark," of the Holy Spirit? The Israelites were to keep their eyes *on the ark* so they would know where to go. In the same way, we need to keep our eyes on the "ark" of God within us and trust that the power and anointing will lead us through places we didn't expect and places we have not been before. We further need to be assured that the ark within is producing the supernatural to accomplish it.

Joshua told them, "You will know which way to go, since you have never been this way before" (Josh. 3:4, NIV). They were to trust that the ark would lead them correctly through uncharted territory. God wants you to know that the presence of His Spirit in you will navigate you accurately and that you can trust it. Watch what Joshua told the people would be the result if they would confidently follow the ark into new places: "The LORD will do wonders among you" (v. 5). If we will trust our ability to operate in the power of God, which is our "ark" of the Holy Spirit, then the outcome will always produce the miraculous power of God!

For some people the unexpected is that they aren't confident to follow the different expressions of the Holy Spirit. Either they can't follow how the Spirit expresses Himself in someone else, or they cannot break out and let God use them in new and unusual ways different from what they are used to. They are only confident with one way of prophesying, one style of worship, or one kind of preaching. God wants us to let His anointing inside of us take us to new places in the Spirit. Just because we haven't seen it or operated in it does not mean that it is not the Lord. So allow the Spirit of God in you to lead you through the unexpected, and know that you can walk on the safe foundation of that water. If you refuse to focus on the boisterous wind around you, you will see yourself forge through powerfully and still be in line with the perfect plan of God for your life.

No Time to Think

Not only did Peter have to deal with the unexpected wind blowing everywhere, but now he also had to address his own fear. The Bible says that Peter was afraid. The fear in him arose when he realized that this level of walking in the Spirit could cause him to drown.

Because the anointing of the Spirit is likened to a river, we can expect that sometimes we will experience rapidly moving water. It means that sometimes you will have to move so quickly that you will fear drowning in the process. The waves will be all around you, but you have to allow the current to carry you. When the prophet Ezekiel saw the vision of the river in Ezekiel 47, the waters were over his head and could not be crossed. When you learn to live from the river of God flowing from the Spirit in you, there will be times when it will seem you are in over your head. The Holy Spirit's waves will move quickly, and you will have to either flow with the current or get back on the shore.

If you have ever watched a news clip on television of a flash flood report or a person who fell into moving water, you can see that there is little that can be done while the person or object just sails helplessly downstream. As you learn how to step into the deeper things of the Spirit, you can't stay on the shore because of the fear of drowning. You don't always have time to "arrange" how you plan to move with the anointing. There may be times the water is moving fast all around you, and you can either stay safely on the shore watching the water or jump into it. If you will train yourself over time to trust the anointing in you, then you will learn how to get into the deeper, fast-moving current of God and not drown in it.

Peter saw the water everywhere and began to be afraid of it. To stay in the current river of God, we have to get over our fear of water. Many Christians are happy to live in a spiritual wading pool. The problem with that is water in a pool is not moving and can become stagnant. This is how so many people and churches get caught up in religious tradition. They started out with tangible power but became comfortable with where they were and never built upon what they had. New places in the Holy Spirit may feel unpredictable at times, but that is what will keep you in the fresh and current moves of God.

Many camps and moves throughout the numerous circles of Christianity have become stagnant with time because they never kept moving. They are content with the songs they sang for the last five years because they were so powerful. So they either sing the same ones year after year, or they only write new ones that have the same musical feel. We have the habit of always trying to "re-create" the same anointing and thus never step into anything fresh. This is why so many moves of God become stale. When a new "current" of the Holy Spirit comes our way, we analyze it instead of flowing in it. We can't be afraid we will move in the fast-moving water of the Spirit. Sometimes you just have to take the plunge! Of course, I am not saying take an "accept anything" approach to spiritual things, but we do need to get beyond our familiar expressions and manifestations when the Holy Spirit is trying to take us into new things. Stay biblical and accountable, but also stay in the fresh depths of God.

A key way the river of the Holy Spirit will flow out of you with new expressions is through the operation of the gifts of the Spirit. There are times when the anointing for it will come upon you suddenly for healing or a prophecy, and the Lord wants you to react to it quickly. You can't spend time reasoning about it.

I remember one time when I was in a special meeting we hosted in our church, and toward the end of praise and worship, I suddenly felt led to prophesy a word. There were so many ministers and visitors there, and I just dismissed it, trying not to add another thing to the service. So I fought the flow of the Spirit and held back, because in my mind I wanted to give our guest speakers plenty of time and not distract from their ministry. Do you know what happened? The speaker began to minister right along the lines of the word the Holy Spirit brought bubbling up out of me. Of course, the anointing of the night was awesome, but I always wondered how it could have even been further enhanced had I just jumped into the river without reasoning myself out of it. Because I paused to think it through, I never jumped into the river; I stayed on the shore where it was safe. When the Holy Spirit moves suddenly, there are times you just have to respond without thinking about it, while at the same time still being skillful enough to know when the setting is right and be able to handle it with manners and in biblical order.

When my husband and I first started ministering together in tongues and interpretation, it seemed somewhat normal and not out of the ordinary of how many other people have ministered along these lines. Then the more we started doing it, the more unusual the expressions became and the faster we had to operate. There have been times it felt like we were in dangerous floodwaters! My husband started running through the auditorium grabbing people and "decreeing" over them in unusual expressions in tongues, and then I had to interpret them. Sometimes the Spirit of the Lord would move so fast we would be out of breath by the time we were done. Now I have had to learn to jump into it. I don't have time to stand on the shore and wonder if I am going to drown in the flow or make a mistake. It's a fast-moving current, and you have to go with the flow.

Now my prophet of a husband is very expressive in how he often ministers in tongues over people, but after learning to trust that "current" in the Spirit, I know how to tap into it. While sometimes it can appear that I could gain the general direction of the interpretation from some of his hand motions, I have found that there is just no time to think that way. I have to just flow with it fast with little time to see or even remember everything and be able to do it with razor-sharp accuracy. It is even more challenging when ministering in a foreign nation where we use a translator. Then we have three people speaking, and I have to pause for the translator and still interpret the word of the Holy Spirit. The best way I have found to flow is without taking the time to think it through; just jump into the river coming out of you. That is why the Bible says it comes from your belly and not your head!

THE FLESH CONNECTION

Once Peter removed his focus from the faith to walk on water, he began to sink. In our walk with the Lord, we are either walking or sinking. There is truthfully no real in-between. We will stay in the Spirit if we keep our eyes on the Holy Spirit in us. However, when our focus is turned back onto ourselves because of life's trials and distractions, we will always find ourselves sinking into a lifestyle that caters to and comforts the flesh. Peter began to sink because his mind was more on his own well-being than on the Lord. If you want to learn how to depend on the anointing within you, then you will have cut your connection to a dependency on your flesh. There are two main reasons that we stay connected to the arm of flesh: (1) for our answers, and (2) for our pleasure.

Answers from the flesh connection

Most of the time we feel safer hearing the opinion of the doctor, the lawyer, the stock report, or just a friend than we do trusting the inward voice of the Holy Ghost. This is because we don't regularly practice hearing, responding, and then seeing the fruit that comes from living from the well of our spirit. A great many believers do not practice learning to hear God this way, yet this is the way the Spirit of God will most often speak to us. Again, we are usually more comfortable with God speaking to us through someone else than we are confident that He will speak directly to us and that we can accurately hear His voice.

God uses people. He uses parents, pastors, and good Christian friends to help us stay pure and accurate in the Spirit. However, people cannot be a substitute for the Spirit of the Lord in our own spirit. It is easy to get caught up in the practice of finding someone to be our resource all the time and forget that God wants to teach us how to find solutions that come from within us. Once we learn how to be confident in getting the answer from the well of the Holy Ghost inside, then it is good to have the safeguards of friends, churches, and family to confirm what we are sensing. Most people would rather just find a prophet and hear God that way instead. They would rather get the healing ministry to pray over them than use the anointing God gave them. Sometimes that is because we truthfully know the Lord inside us is going to say something we don't want to hear, and so we find people who will tell us what we would rather hear instead.

The other scenario is many just think a human opinion is more reliable than the Holy Spirit because we can hear and see it with physical ears and eyes. It feels safer for us to stay on the shore than to walk on the water—the water of the Spirit. It may make us feel better to depend on a fleshly solution to find direction or to meet our needs, but the Bible gives some real insight into what happens when we do that and, in turn, what happens when we trust the Lord.

First, Jeremiah 17:5–6 says, "Thus saith the LORD; Cursed be the man that trusted in man, and maketh flesh his arm, and whose heart departeth from the LORD. For he shall be like the heath in the desert, and shall not see when good cometh; but shall inhabit the parched places in the wilderness, in a salt land and not inhabited." Now these scriptures give us a lot to digest. Notice it says trusting the flesh is the same as departing from the Lord. By always needing a human solution, we will find ourselves leaving God out of everything. Then we get angry when we feel He has deserted us somehow. Yet He is inside us and wants to participate in everything we do. God uses people, but He *alone* wants to be the object of your desire and your dependency for everything. You go to Him right down on the inside of the well of your spirit. You practice hearing, sensing, and trusting. The more you do, the more you will see Him move through your life that way. Then when a piece of bad news comes across the television or from the doctor's office, you aren't moved by it. You aren't going to sink because you have trusted in God, the fountain of living water. The only way to do it is through a lifestyle of practice that doesn't quit because of a mistake or two.

Then these verses in Jeremiah also tell us the result a flesh dependency will bring us. It says we become like a "heath in the desert." A heath is tumbleweed, and tumbleweeds will blow from thing to thing and are not rooted to anything. So many people in the church are tumbling from place to place trying to find answers, new excitement, fulfillment, preferences, and opinions. We need to settle down and become rooted and stable. Tumbleweeds are quite comfortable without water. A dependence on natural solutions will make us void of the water of the Spirit, and we won't notice that we are missing out on the supernatural things of God.

Many people can't draw from the well of their spirit because they have allowed it to dry up—they never use it. They want to draw from the well in everyone else instead. My spiritual well can help another believer, and it should do that, but we also should encourage each other to learn how to drink from our own well in the Spirit. Then we can use the well within us to relieve the thirst of those who really need it—the lost.

Then verse 6 above says that they "shall not see when good cometh." Have you ever known a Christian like that? They can't seem to find blessing in anything, or they always have a problem to solve. Even when they receive a blessing, they can only keep their mind on all their problems. When we depend on the flesh for answers, the Bible says we won't recognize the good when it does come. In other words, even if the answer is in front of you, you will not see it! I wonder how many miracles and breakthroughs we have missed because our eyes were so much on man to come through for us that God's power passed us by.

Lastly, verse 6 says that a flesh-dependent person will live in a dry place. In fact, in the vision of Ezekiel 47, which is all about the well of the Holy Spirit, we find in verse 11 that the miry land where the water of the Spirit does not flow will be given to salt. Salt speaks of judgment and curse; it is also the righteous side of God that demands a just and higher standard. When something is given over to salt, it ceases to feel refreshed. God has given us every way to avoid a dry spiritual experience by the river of power from the Spirit of God who lives in us. In that river, His righteousness (salt) is soothed and relieved by His mercy (water). When we depend on those waters for the answers we need, we will find life and power. Our relationship to God will stay fresh, and we don't have to search for the arm of flesh to sustain us.

Let's continue and look at the wonderful things the Bible says will happen by making life in the Spirit our way of living. Jeremiah 17:7–8 says, "Blessed is the man that trusteth in the LORD, and whose hope the LORD is. For he shall be as a tree planted by the *waters*, and that speadeth out her roots by the *river*, and shall not see when heat cometh, but her leaf shall be green; and shall not be careful in the year of drought, neither shall cease from yielding fruit" (emphasis added). What a powerful passage! This is the result of relying on what Jesus said would come from the well of your own spirit (John 7:37–39). It says you will be rooted, which means stable and secure. When the heat of life comes your way, you won't even notice it. Does that even sound possible? The Bible says it is possible. It goes on to say that you won't even be fearful at the sign of a coming drought. Why? *Because you have an internal fountain of life that streams from the Spirit of the living God Himself, and He is never changed by a dry season.*

If your trust for answers is always on the earth, then you are susceptible to drought. But if you know you carry an internal source of powerful water, then you don't have to fear it! That is why the verse ends saying you will never stop bearing fruit. How can we be fruitless when we are never dry? In that atmosphere you enjoy blessing after blessing. Answers to prayer come, and you hear the voice of God. The gifts of the Spirit will work for you, and power will flow through your hands. On every side you can't help but yield powerful fruit.

Pleasure from the flesh connection

The other reason we stay connected to our flesh is to fulfill natural pleasure. Now that does not mean God does not want us to physically enjoy life. The Bible says in 1 Timothy 6:17 that God gives us all things richly to enjoy. The pleasure of flesh becomes sinful when it wants to draw us away from life in the Spirit. The Bible says in Galatians 5:17, "For the flesh lusteth against the Spirit, and the Spirit against the flesh: and these are contrary the one to the other: so that ye cannot do the things that ye would." Our flesh is constantly trying to pull us out of the river of the Spirit because it makes us feel that it is more comfortable on the shore. I am sure when Peter was standing out on the water in the storm, he was not as comfortable as the other eleven guys in the ship. Flesh always wants comfort and pleasure, and once we taste something that we like, it is hard to live without it.

One way that our flesh pulls us out of the river of the Spirit is by making us tired. It feels so good to lie in bed the extra hours in the morning rather than get up and pray. It can be hard! My mouth is usually still stuck together from sleeping, and it's a challenge to make it move! Then if we are not careful, we develop the habit of sleeping late and not praying. There are many ways our flesh's need for pleasure will pull us out of the Spirit. The verse in Galatians 5:17 says that it will draw you so hard that you almost can't resist it. It says, "That ye cannot do the things that ye would."

Habits, sins, additions, distractions, money, occupations…these are all things that keep us connected to a fleshly lifestyle. Many of us don't want to truly live fleshly; it is just that the pull of the flesh is so strong sometimes that we find ourselves falling into it. The apostle Paul dealt with the struggles against his own flesh in Romans chapters 7 and 8. In that latter part of chapter 7 he talks about the difficult challenge of trying to do what is right, but then in Romans 8:1, he gives a key solution: "There is therefore now no condemnation to them which are in Christ Jesus, who walk not after the flesh, but after the Spirit." Then Galatians 5:16 reiterates it by saying, "This I say then, Walk in the Spirit, and ye shall not fulfil the lust of the flesh."

The answer to dealing with the flesh seems so simple it is almost disappointing. The only way to overcome the desires of our flesh is to cut them off by staying in the river of the Holy Spirit. Notice that it says if you choose to walk in the Spirit you *won't* fulfill the flesh. In other words, by doing spiritual things like praying in tongues and reading the Bible regularly, you are automatically not as drawn to fleshly pleasure. The Spirit starts to take over—again it's supernatural in nature. This is because the well of your spirit grows stronger, and its power begins to flow over fleshly desires.

However, you can't expect to quickly pray and read the Bible while your flesh is being tempted. You need to do it when you are not under attack—and make a habit of it. Then when the devil places temptation before you that your flesh would normally enjoy, you will have a flood of spiritual water to draw from and fall into. It is nothing short of the miraculous power of God on you.

Unlike Peter, who sank when he didn't feel he could depend on the water, we can overcome our dependency on fleshly things by drawing on the Holy Spirit within. Peter must have learned the importance of drawing from the well of the Spirit as the answer to address the flesh. He later wrote about those who depend on the flesh as their source in 2

Peter 2:10–17. He said, "But chiefly them that walk after the flesh…these are wells without water." Their flesh connection caused them to jump out of the river of the Spirit, leaving them dry. By continually drawing from the well inside us, the flood of the Spirit will cut off the flesh connection and make us supernatural Christians.

Is There Anything Besides Water?

We read in Matthew 14:30 that once Peter began to sink, he began to cry and holler. Suddenly he didn't want to do this anymore. That walking on the water experience was over for him! Like many of us, he probably wanted to do something else right then. I don't know if he wanted to escape and just go eat or go to bed. Maybe he stayed up all night and thought over what had just happened to him. We don't know for sure, but we can be certain he didn't want another "water" experience for a while.

This is a common response for when we feel like we failed at something or when we try to take a step of faith, but the results don't turn out the way we expected. That is right where Peter was that day. He expected to walk on water and experience the supernatural successfully, but he sank before he reached his goal. At that point somebody was going to hear about it because he cried out!

When we try to walk in the miraculous and feel like we have failed, most of the time someone will hear about it. Usually we begin to talk about our frustration, and the very first thing we begin to say is, "Well, I remember one time when I prayed for something like that, it didn't turn out so good." The tendency is to complain about it, talk about, and cry over it. We get vocal about it just as Peter did. I can usually tell when people haven't trained themselves to trust the power of God in them by the way they talk. They will eventually speak about their struggles more than their victories. For most of us, once we begin to cry out to the Lord about our frustration, our next usual action is to decide we are done trying to operate in the "water-walking" anointing. We want something besides water.

It isn't always easy to learn how to step out and walk in the power of God. The children of Israel began to follow the Lord out of Egypt with a powerful supernatural beginning, but they became frustrated with the way they were being led. Numbers 21:4 says, "And they journeyed from mount Hor by the way of the Red sea, to compass the land of Edom: and the soul of the people was much discouraged because of the way." There are two main reasons we look for something other than the water of the Spirit when we feel discouraged.

Reason #1: "Why did I fail?"

Perhaps Peter asked, "Why did I fail? What did I do wrong?" He was probably like most of us who would have questioned it. When we don't receive the healing or miracle we expected, we start to ask why. I have dealt with several people who have prayed and perhaps either someone they love died anyway or something specific didn't work out right. These situations left them disillusioned.

In one case, I was talking to the Lord about a person's situation, and the Lord said something powerful to me. He said, "Have your children ever asked you a question about something that, as a parent, you could not answer for them right then?" I said, "Well, yes, Lord, of course." Obviously as parents, we can't tell our kids everything they want to know because they are not mature enough to handle some of the answers to the questions they ask. We try to give them the kindergarten version, but that doesn't always satisfy them.

It only raises more questions for which the answers are too much for them to grasp at their particular ages, even if you did try to explain. I have had to sometimes frankly tell my children that I was giving them all I could and that they would understand some things better as they get older.

In this case, the Lord was revealing to me that as our heavenly Father, He cannot tell us everything about our situation, because if He did, we wouldn't be mature enough to handle all the spiritual truth of it. Either it would be too much to bear, or we wouldn't understand it. It would only serve to confuse us further as God's children who are all growing in our understanding of spiritual things. Now that doesn't mean we have to wait until we get to heaven for the answers. It just means that God wants us to grow into them so we can handle them.

Since receiving this revelation, I always encourage people that if they have come through a tragic or disappointing situation and it didn't seem like a miracle manifested, don't get out of the water when you don't know why everything seemed to fail. Perhaps God cannot answer why about everything right now, but as you grow and stay close to Him, the day will come when the answers will begin to become clear to you. If you get angry and decide you will never walk on the water again, then God may never be able to communicate the answers to you.

As I watched this person for whom things seemed to go wrong despite their prayers, I saw that, over time, God began to unfold what he needed to know. Today he is experiencing the supernatural and living in total victory. So even when there are loose ends to the answers, don't quit trusting the water of the Spirit to work through you. Believe that, no matter what, you still house the miraculous power of God. Don't replace the anointing of the Holy Spirit by looking for something else. Peter may have failed when he walked on the water, but the day came when he learned to successfully operate in the power of the Holy Ghost because he didn't quit.

Reason #2: Water isn't exciting to drink anymore.

The other reason many people quit operating in the Spirit is because they have been around the church and "spiritual things" for so long they are bored. Human nature loves to see something new all of the time. We like to be awed and entertained. Know that walking in the supernatural isn't always entertaining. Sometimes it is real warfare to have God's best in your life. You have to fight for it. In fact, the miracles of the Bible often created persecution.

When people become bored with a daily commitment of praying in the Spirit, reading the Bible, or decreeing the word of the Lord, many don't stay committed to it. It is mostly because using the well of your spirit is done by yourself. Only a small percentage of the Spirit's power are the miracles and glorious praise we all love in corporate ministry at a conference or crusade. Most of our spiritual power is cultivated when we are alone, and this is where people get bored. Most of our worship to God is done alone and without the help of musicians. It is just you and God and your voice. In this setting "spiritual water" can begin to feel like it is not the beverage of choice anymore. It isn't always exciting, so we want something besides water.

Now I said earlier that we have to be quick to flow with the Holy Spirit when He moves fast, or we risk getting stuck in the past. The other side to that is some people are so busy jumping from thing to thing around the body of Christ that they aren't walking in a stable daily life from their well. If it doesn't keep them entertained, they are bored with it because they associate the supernatural things of God with the spectacular. What we have to remember is the supernatural often begins with the ordinary, and many don't want to walk out that phase. Think of Jesus being born in a manger. Something so ordinary and unassuming was Earth's greatest miracle in the making. You can't replace the genuine supernatural with expecting the spectacular. If you do, you could end up following the wrong thing in order to stay engaged and entertained.

Instead of drawing daily from their well of water, some Christians are busy trying to get in on the latest "thing" going on around Christendom. Participation in those things is great, but you have to drink daily from you own well or you will not live stable as a Christian. You will always need a spiritual "high" to keep you going. It is like the difference between eating green beans and drinking a milk shake. Some Christians only want to go from place to place drinking spiritual milk shakes, living on a spiritual sugar high. Listen, I love milk shakes too, but I know that to be a healthy believer I need spiritual green beans and a daily diet that makes me strong and releases the anointing in me. I may not always want to eat it or even chew on it, but in the end it is what makes me walk consistently and securely in the anointing through every situation.

This is called living from the well of your spirit every day. It may not feel very exciting, entertaining, or even taste good sometimes to draw the same water every morning, but it will be the very thing that positions you for the true supernatural things of God. In the Old Testament, the children of Israel got tired of the manna God gave them. They got bored going out every morning with the same baskets, to the same fields, and having to walk around and collect the same strange food they had been eating every day. Remember how they started crying about the manna and demanded quail to eat (Num. 11)? I mean, imagine if you went to the grocery store and all they had on the shelves were Wheaties! Wheaties taste good, but if you had to eat them for breakfast, lunch, and dinner for days on end, you might not like Wheaties anymore.

This is what happens to many people with the spiritual water inside them. They quit using it because it is too troublesome to fill it, draw from it, and use it, and doing it over and over gets mundane. It ceases to feel flavorful and exciting, so they would rather do something else and then get a drink from someone else's well should they get thirsty.

When Peter saw himself sinking in the water, he cried about it and was ready to quit. You don't have to quit. Yes, it takes commitment to depend on the Spirit of God that is in you. Yes, it takes a daily dedication to draw from that well. You might wake up some mornings and even cry about it because it looks like nothing is happening. However, just keep on drawing from the well, and you will eventually learn to walk on your own provision of spiritual water.

I Can't, So Lord, Save Me!

As soon as Peter felt like he wasn't going to succeed in walking on the water, he asked the Lord to save him. I have prayed a few desperate prayers like this too, the kind where you sort of hit your knees before you even make it all the way into the room and just skid across the room screaming, "Lord, save me!" Have you ever said, "I just can't do this anymore"? You can feel sometimes like you are so *un*anointed that you want to give up altogether. You don't want to pray in the Spirit or confess the Word of God. You just want God to *please* do something now!

In Matthew 17:14–21, Jesus's disciples came to Him with just one of those situations. They had just tried to manifest a miracle and cast a demon out of a young man who was possessed. Not knowing what to do, and probably with the disciples present, the father decided to bring the boy to Jesus in one of those "Lord, save me" moments. This story makes me laugh because you would think Jesus would respond with the usual way we expect Him to respond to us when we pull a "Lord, save me." We expect Him to give us an understanding pat on the back and His loving eyes to say, "My sweet child, I know how you feel." This was not at all how Jesus responded to the Twelve. Not even close! In verse 17, He boldly said, "O faithless and perverse generation, how long shall I be with you? how long shall I suffer you? bring him hither to me."

How embarrassing! Here were the leaders of Jesus's ministry standing with a multitude of people, and Jesus is making this kind of statement in their moment of desperation. Basically He is saying that He is tired of putting up with them! Now this wasn't the only time Jesus responded this way to His disciple's moments of apparent failure to operate in supernatural power against a problem. In fact, when Peter began to sink into the water earlier in Matthew 14, Jesus responded in a similar way. It makes me wonder how the Lord is often responding to us when we try to step out in faith and then give up. Why would He change for us?

Be encouraged, all hope is not lost. Jesus was not trying to kick them while they were down, and He isn't trying to kick us while we are down either. Instead, Jesus was trying to get them to continue using their anointing rather than resort to "Lord, save me."

Now there is something very key that I want you to see. In both accounts, Matthew 14, with Peter and the water, and

Matthew 17, with the disciples and the demon, Jesus reached out and saved them both times. However, both times He corrected them for an attitude of "I can't." Yes, Jesus helped Peter back to the safe boat, and yes, He helped the disciples get rid of the demon, but that was not what He wanted to do. He wanted them to use their own faith and the power He gave them already. He not only wanted it, but He also expected them to use it right in the middle of their adversity.

Then in Matthew 17:20–21, Jesus taught them a valuable lesson about manifesting the power of God when they asked why they couldn't produce a miracle. I have read these verses many times, and perhaps you have also, but I want you to read it again very carefully to see Jesus's answer. He said, "Because of your unbelief: for verily I say unto you, If ye have faith as a grain of mustard seed, ye shall say unto this mountain, Remove hence to yonder place; and it shall remove; and nothing shall be impossible unto you. Howbeit this kind goeth not out but by prayer and fasting." Jesus taught them five powerful things that will help us understand why it seems like the anointing isn't working and how to use it, so then we don't find ourselves continuing to cry, "Lord, save me." Instead, we can rise up in the power of the Spirit.

1. *Your unbelief.* The disciples didn't think they had the power to do it, so they quit, just as Peter did and just how we often do also.

2. *Not letting your faith grow.* The verse says, "If ye have faith as a grain of mustard seed..." Seeds grow. They seem useless at first and may appear that they are producing nothing, but if you keep them in the ground, they will manifest. The disciples didn't let their faith continue to grow in the

power of God that they possessed. Instead they quit when it looked like failure.

3. *Not speaking forth anything.* "Ye shall say..." Jesus said you have to speak something. Perhaps the disciples weren't speaking, or Jesus probably wouldn't have brought it up. He said you have to speak to the problem, not talk to God about the problem. That is the trouble Paul fell into with his thorn in the flesh (2 Cor. 12). He wanted the Lord to save him. Jesus said you have to tell the mountain to leave, not yell, "Lord, save me."

4. *Not believing that "nothing shall be impossible to you."* Notice He said, "...to you." That means you have the power within you to perform the impossible. Is your situation impossible today? You can overcome it if you believe the Spirit of the Lord in you is powerful enough to do the impossible.

5. *Not keeping a regular lifestyle of fasting and prayer.* "This kind goeth not out but by prayer and fasting." Whether He was referring to the actual demon or any mountain in your life, it takes regular prayer and fasting to keep your river flowing and active for the times in life you will have to depend on it.

Jesus would not have been helping His disciples had He catered to their feelings during the moment of their failure. It is not because the Lord doesn't care when we are hurting, frustrated, or feeling like a failure. His whole motive is that He wants us to rise up from the well of our spirit and let the river of anointing flood the situation we are facing so that we don't have to struggle anymore.

God's real compassion is in the fact that He does not want you to succumb to failure. He won't allow it, not when He has given you all of Himself to reside within. He wants you to rise up, walk on the water of the Spirit, cast out demons, move mountains, and live strong from the well of anointing you received when you were filled with the Holy Ghost.

I love what Jesus finally said to Peter in Matthew 14:31, "…wherefore didst thou doubt?" My first response to that is, "Lord, can't you see that Peter doubted because of everything around him?" Jesus *never* even acknowledged to Peter that he should have had one valid reason to doubt the anointing for one tiny second. He didn't even compliment Peter once for trying at all. As far as Jesus seemed to be concerned, it was as if the boisterous wind was nonexistent, a moot point. I think Jesus knows something about the *dunamis* power of God that we do not know. He knows it will work, no matter what is blowing around us, and that *dunamis* power has been downloaded into us! Glory to God!

SURE, NOW THE WIND STOPS!

Finally, in verse 32 of Matthew 14, the story of Peter's amazing experience of walking on the anointing ends with, "And when they were come into the ship, the *wind ceased*" (emphasis added). Not only did Jesus refuse to acknowledge to Peter that the wind was actually blowing really hard before, but now that the weather was more conducive for Peter to succeed they were in the safety of the boat. How unfair! Sure, now when it would have been easier and after he was out of the water, the wind around him stopped blowing. Isn't that how it works? When you are living on top spiritually and feel like you can overcome every demon of hell, nothing is blowing in your life. Right when you feel ready to trust the anointing and walk on water, all is going great.

Without question, the wind ceased in verse 32 as soon as they jumped out of the water, only to make an enormous spiritual point. You and I need to know how to rely on the river of our spirit when the storm is blowing because that is when you need it. If you don't learn to use it under pressure, when you want to die and fall apart, you will never truly know what it means to live from the well of your own spirit. That is where the anointing is, and that is the place for the greatest supernatural occurrences.

I want to encourage you to rise up today and put your foot down in front of the devil. Let him know that you are not a quitter. Tell him that you refuse to jump out of the river of the Holy Spirit. You are an anointed vessel of the Most High, empowered with His Spirit. Jesus is standing there watching you use your equipment. He knows you can do it. Go ahead and prophesy to yourself. Shout out in other tongues. Speak the Word of God and command miracles to produce themselves from within you. Jesus won't let you sink, but He will encourage to you stand strong on the surface of stable water coming out of you. You can live from the well of your spirit today, but whatever you do, don't jump out of the river.

Chapter Seven

PRAYER THAT WORKS MIRACLES

E VERYONE HAS A different preference when it comes
to prayer and how he or she feels is the best way to
connect with God. In this chapter, I want to explore
some expressions of prayer that will help you draw on the
anointing inside of you. You will be extremely encouraged
and will receive renewed confidence that you are being effective in your prayers. The important thing is to remember that
you don't want your prayer life to become mundane, never
growing and changing. You want your prayer life to be fresh,
exciting, and even explosive in the Spirit. We all want our
prayers to be effective, and anyone who is full of the Spirit
has the anointing to have powerful prayers that produce
miracles.

We can arrive at places in prayer where they just flow.
We don't have to force them. Our prayers can even become
prophetic in nature. What I mean by that is that they actually become the heart of the Holy Spirit pouring out of your
words and expressions. You don't have to think of what to
pray; the prayers begin to rush out of you. Your words of
prayer and the heart of the Spirit begin to "gel." They become
one heart and a unified flow.

Other than Jesus, one of the men in the Bible we think
of when it comes to prayer is the prophet Elijah. From his

life we can learn some amazing prayer principles about how prayer can come out of the river of our spirit. Let's look at some characteristics about the way he prayed that we can use to enhance our own life of supernatural prayer. James 5:16–18 says, "The effectual fervent prayer of a righteous man availeth much. Elias [Elijah] was a man subject to like passions as we are, and he prayed earnestly that it might not rain: and it rained not on the earth by the space of three years and six months. And he prayed again, and the heaven gave rain, and the earth brought forth her fruit."

There are four main ingredients in these verses, which if added to your prayer life will keep you building in prayer and help you connect to the power of God inside of you. We need all of them, not just some of them, for our prayers to be anointed and flowing. I will list them briefly here and then study them throughout the chapter.

1. Accuracy—"effectual" prayer
2. Expression—"fervent" prayer
3. Intimacy/relationship—"righteous man" and "like passions"
4. Consistency—"prayed earnestly" and "prayed again"

BULL'S-EYE ACCURACY IN PRAYER

Several years ago, we were at a prayer meeting in our church, and we were praying that the Lord would use the ministry more effectively to touch lives in our city. The Lord directed us to begin to pray in such a way that our prayers would have "bull's-eye" accuracy. We knew that the Holy Spirit wanted to develop specific prayers that were going to be like instruments of warfare targeted toward building certain key parts of the church's vision. We were paving the way for it to happen. It went along with Isaiah 49:2–3: "And he hath made my mouth like a sharp sword; in the shadow of his hand hath he hid me, and made me a polished shaft; in his quiver hath he hid me; and said unto me, Thou are my servant, O Israel, in whom I will be glorified."

After that time of prayer, we were amazed at the number of breakthroughs we experienced in our ministry. As believers, we sometimes pray randomly, just repeating things, not really thinking about what we are saying. To have effective prayers, our praying should be calculated with biblical and Spirit-led accuracy. These kinds of prayer are like swords in the Spirit. They shoot out, and something just "clicks" when you pray them. It is one of those times when you just know you hit the target and don't walk away wondering if you received the answer. God wants our mouth, our prayers, to be like sharp swords.

In James 5:16, we see the word *effectual.* This verse is telling us that it is effectual prayer that avails much. The Amplified Bible describes it by saying that it is prayer that "makes tremendous power available." I want to make tremendous power available in my prayers, don't you? Effectual prayer is accurate, targeted prayer that is done with action. In the Greek, it is the word *energeo,* which means to be "efficient, full of energy, and to display working activity." In other words, when you hear someone pray with effectual prayer, you don't have to doubt it is working because there is energy behind it. You can sense and feel power on it just the way you turn on a light bulb. You can obviously tell the light is on.

One part of having prayer that works is praying accurately according to the Bible. Rather than just pray whatever we think and feel, it is necessary to find out what God's will is for the situation and bring all our prayers in line with it. For example, if all the parts and filaments of a light bulb are not accurately put together inside, it will not work when you try to turn the light on. Prayer is the same way. God has a certain way of thinking when it comes to things in our lives, and we need to align with them. He does not adjust to us; we should adjust to Him.

The best example is when it comes to prayer for physical healing. You may feel terrible in your body and want to cry to the Lord about how bad things are going for you. However, a more effectual way to pray is to find out the Lord's promise about your healing from Scripture and pray in agreement with God. It is like having a light bulb that works rather than one that is burned out. This doesn't mean you cannot cry out to the Lord in your time of adversity, because Scripture refers to many people crying out to God this way. What you need, however, in order to stay accurate in prayer, is to then place the focus of your prayer back to a confident trust in God and His promises.

When you make a habit of praying this way every time you pray, you will learn one way of prayer from the river of your spirit. You plug into the Holy Spirit's way, the source of power in you, because you are now agreeing with the Lord's opinion. Instead of trying to swim upstream, you are flowing *with* the current. Remember that when the power of the Holy Spirit flows out of you like a river, it contains miracles, blessings, and answers to prayer. Accurate prayer will help you flow in all those things.

Suddenly instead of praying random, disconnected prayers, you are grabbing hold of the blessing that God has already placed in the river of your spirit. A new energy and confidence will come to your prayer life. It keeps you from feeling like you are always climbing uphill. It brings you to a conclusive result because you are targeting what you need with what God has already promised.

EXPRESSIVE PRAYER THAT LOOSES

James 5:16 also uses the word *fervent*. This word comes from the same Greek word as *effectual* (*energeo*), but it gives another side to describing this kind of prayer. *Effectual* speaks of actively working prayer, while *fervent* is the side of the word that shows expression. Personally, I love expressive, active prayer! You don't fall asleep with this kind of prayer.

For some reason in most of Christianity, we have created very still, quiet, and almost motionless prayer settings and made them the most common expression. That is a legitimate form of prayer expression, but it is only one of them. There are many other expressions in prayer, and they are more than just a mere personality preference or style. There are expressions in prayer that loose spiritual prison bars, change our outlook, and open the heavens. We need to explore the expressive side of prayer so we can flow from the river of the Holy Spirit in whatever way He wants to manifest Himself.

God created human expression for a reason. Facial expressions, voice tones, and physical movements are all ways we express ourselves every single day. You can often tell what a person is thinking just by their expressions. It is like the old saying "Actions speak louder than words." Those actions could be expressions that come out even when you aren't saying a word. In fact, your outward expressions often reveal if you truly mean what you are saying. People can say one thing from their mouth, but their face and body language gives them away. You can tell they didn't mean what they said.

Expression is a part of normal everyday life, and we don't even think about it, but some have a little more trouble with bringing definitive expressions into prayer. It is as if we feel as though expressive prayer might bother God because He may think it isn't reverent. But we forget He is an expressive God. He is the creator of outward expression, and He does not want us to come to Him in a lifeless, unexpressive way. Nearly all examples of prayer and worship in the Bible were very expressive. There were emotions on them. There was bodily action in them.

As I said earlier, God is not afraid of prayer even if it gets loud sometimes. Most prayers in the Bible were either loud, or they were very expressive with someone lying prostrate, clapping, dancing, lifting their hands, or even crying out. Jesus prayed so intently in the Garden of Gethsemane that His sweat became like drops of blood (Luke 22:44). I believe that not only was that a picture of what He was about to do in shedding His precious blood, but it was also something the intensity of His prayers created. Hebrews 5:7 says, "…in the days of his [Jesus] flesh…he had offered up prayers and supplications with strong crying and tears unto him that was able to save him from death." In other words, He offered up intense, fervent prayer.

Elijah was a man of intense, fervent prayer. He did many things when he prayed that revealed that his prayers were not only heartfelt but also effectual, fervent prayers. On one occasion his fervent expressive way of praying not only bound the rain for three years, but it also later loosed the heavens until it rained. In 1 Kings 17:1, the Bible says Elijah prophesied to Ahab that it wouldn't rain. Even though he was speaking the word of the Lord, the Bible says he prayed expressively to bring it to pass. James 5:17 says, "He prayed earnestly that it might not rain: and it rained not." This indicates that this mighty prophet of God didn't just prophesy about the rain, but he also *prayed* so that it would not rain. When it says that he prayed earnestly, it means he prayed in a way that was not only very worshipful and expressive but also continual.

Some translations indicate that he kept praying that it would not rain for the entire three years while the rain was stopped. That is why, even though something is prophesied, prayer must still follow and be involved in bringing about the desired outcome.

Now watch how he prayed for the rain to return in 1 Kings 18:41–42. "And Elijah said unto Ahab, Get thee up, eat and drink; for there is a sound of abundance of rain. So Ahab went up to eat and to drink. And Elijah went up to the top of Carmel; and he cast himself down upon the earth, and put his face between his knees." His same expressive fashion in prayer is now shown as he prayed with his head between his knees. You don't get the impression that his way of praying was motionless and reserved. Instead it seems he had a way of praying that was very demonstrative, so much so that the Bible drew attention to it.

Elijah also prayed in an expressive, demonstrative way when he prayed for the son of the widow of Zarephath in 1 Kings 17:17–22, who had died. The prophet took the woman's dead son and laid him on his own personal bed. He began to cry to the Lord in an almost angry and frustrated way, and then three times he stretched himself across the body of the boy, saying, "Lord, let this child's soul come into him again." The Bible said that the Lord heard and the boy revived. I am sure that to the average onlooker his actions were very strange. That is because things of the Spirit can look strange to those who are not after spiritual things. However, this prophet of God was earmarked by demonstrative and expressive prayers.

Elisha too must have learned this impartation of expressive prayer from his spiritual father, Elijah. We find an almost identical story about him when he also raised a dead boy to life. In 2 Kings 4, the Shunammite woman, to whom he prophesied would have a son, ran to him because her son whom he had prophesied about had died.

In verses 29–31, Elisha told his servant to go place his staff upon the boy, but the boy didn't respond. So Elisha went to the house where the boy was laying. The Bible says in verse 33, "He went in therefore, and shut the door upon them twain [he and the boy], and prayed unto the LORD." Now we don't know for sure how long he was in that room praying, but we see there was some unusual expression in his prayers. In verses 34–35, Elisha went to the child and stretched himself across the body of the dead boy, face-to-face, mouth to mouth. The boy's body warmed up, but he still didn't wake up. Lastly, he went into the house and paced back and forth and then went back and stretched himself across the boy again. This time the boy began to sneeze and woke up. In his case, the Bible doesn't give any reference to the words that came out of Elisha's mouth while he prayed, but like Elijah's story, it definitely tells us something about the expression of the prayers.

I believe there is something significant about fervent and expressive prayers. This type of prayer will release you into a new dimension in your prayer life. It looses things, just as it loosed the rain when Elijah prayed. Demonstration and expression are like the fuel behind the words. They cause something inside of your spirit to unlock and flow. If you are shy or even slightly uncertain about expressing yourself in prayer, I encourage you to practice stepping out in small ways at home. Begin by making yourself pray aloud above your normal voice tone sometimes. Begin to walk around while you pray. You don't have to scream, but small steps of putting your body into prayer will release you and create a new flow in prayer. This is part of learning to pray in the river of God. Fervent, expressive prayer will unlock the flow and power of God in you and open your faith to the supernatural anointing.

I have had times in prayer when I was just sitting on my couch praying quietly, but then I have gotten up and continued by pacing and praying with a louder voice and more expression. There is something about it that ignites my faith and helps me begin to believe in my own prayers in a new dimension. Expression has a way of helping you become settled on what you believe, no matter what it is you are expressing yourself about. For example, if you attend a football game and watch the way fans cheer, it is the louder and more expressive ones who give you the sense that they are really behind their team. Expression helps us draw faith out of our hearts.

Intimate Relationship, Not a Business Appointment

Often the reason we have trouble with creating a flow of prayer where we pour out from the anointing of the Spirit is because many people treat their prayer time like a business meeting on the calendar. "OK, God, I have one hour. This is what I have on the agenda to go over, and I hope You are hearing all of it." There is no heartfelt relationship behind it. It is just a prayer list. There is nothing wrong with having a prayer list, but your prayer has to be much more than just completing a list. Many people's prayer list sounds something like this: "Lord, thank You for today. Bless so-and-so. Help me do what is right. Bless my family, and forgive me of my sins. Amen." Now we stretch the prayer out a bit more than that, but that is still the essence of it. It feels like we are reciting a fax or Internet task list.

I attended a large prayer luncheon many years ago where a group of businesspeople and church leaders were all taking turns praying around all the different tables. They were so proper about it. For about forty-five whole minutes, the monotone sound never changed once as people tried to impress one another with their long lists of prayer requests. The "1-2-3" lists got lengthier and even more monotone. You could feel people getting fidgety trying to stay awake. I could feel myself fading in and out of a sleepy state, trying so hard to fight it off! I am sure there was one person who actually did fall asleep. When it was finally over, you could hear little sighs of stretching and almost relief fill the room. That was not a picture of Bible prayer; it was religious prayer. There was no flow because there was no real relationship or intimacy with God that came out in it. It felt like nothing more than empty recitations.

Then a few years later I was in another prayer retreat with several ministers, and some of the prayers being prayed by different ones were similar to what I just described above— perhaps a little livelier but not much. Then one missionary got up and prayed over the lunch as it was served. Now keep in mind it was the lunch prayer! Expecting it to be the most brief and rehearsed prayer of all, everyone reverently folded their hands. However, as this missionary prayed, he started out calmly thanking God for the food, and then his prayer went over into the anointing. He began to worship and thank

God in a way that you could feel something. His prayer came out like a machine gun. You could tell this man made a habit of connecting with God on a supernatural level. Truthfully, it was the first jolt we probably felt all day. However, as he prayed and his voice got louder and his words came out faster, you could feel people getting nervous and fidgety. People just aren't used to expressive prayer like that, especially over the lunch!

Prayer that comes from the river of your spirit comes from a living relationship. It is like when you are so excited that you get to talk to a good friend. You can't help it as the words and excitement begin to just pour out of you. You are so excited to talk, share, and recall special times. James 5:16–17 again gives us some clues to the relationship part of prayer that gives your prayers effervescence. They just bubble out of your river flow.

Verse 16 uses the phrase "prayer of a righteous man." Now that verse is not trying to indicate that prayer only becomes powerful when you are perfect. The New Life Version says, "The prayer from the heart of a man right with God has much power." This is a heart that is connected to God in relationship. Anytime a relationship between two individuals is right or on good terms, it is the result of the continued communication and friendship. There is no awkwardness when you speak to your friend because you talk regularly and recognize his or her voice and feelings. You can speak to one another with ease. This is how God wants our prayer life to become—a flow from a relationship that is filled with life and excitement.

James 5:17 shows this further when it says, "Elias [Elijah] was a man subject to *like passions* as we are" (emphasis added). Here was this mighty prophet who accomplished so many incredible things, but the Bible says he was no different from us. What made his prayers special is that they were heartfelt and birthed out of a personal relationship to God. He meant his prayers; he didn't just recite them. That is why many of us never find a river or flow in prayer because we often just recite prayers rather than mean them. But we are no different from Elijah, and we can have the same "in" with God and see incredible results in prayer!

John 15:5–8 says, "I am the Vine, you are the branches. When you're joined with me and I with you, the relation intimate and organic, the harvest is sure to be abundant. Separated, you can't produce a thing. Anyone who separates from me is deadwood, gathered up and thrown on the bonfire. But if you make yourselves at home with me and my words are at home in you, you can be sure that whatever you ask will be listened to and acted upon. This is how my Father shows who he is—when you produce grapes, when you mature as my disciples" (THE MESSAGE).

Your prayer life will flow like a river out of you when it is built upon relationship. You don't have to try to work up things to say. They just start spilling and overflowing from your heart. This is another dimension of praying from the well of your spirit. Like Elijah, we will get answers and results in this flow of prayer and the anointing. It ceases to be just words; it is something that bubbles and spills from inside of you. Once that happens, you are moving and flowing with the Holy Spirit, and you will find that there is power behind what you pray. You can ask what you desire, and the Lord will grant it to you.

THE DAILY DIP IN THE RIVER

The next way we create a flow in the river of prayer is by consistency. We need a daily dip into the rivers of prayer to stay fresh in the things of the Spirit. Otherwise, we get dry and stale, often without knowing it has happened. For example, without the plumbing in your house being used regularly, it can struggle to work properly. The pipes can fill with air, parts can corrode, and the water can begin to be discolored or take on a funny taste. Regular use keeps the plumbing working properly and the water tasting fresh.

This is the case with prayer. Notice that James 5:18 says, "And he [Elijah] prayed again." He didn't just pray once and then forget about prayer until he was in some sort of pickle. This was not the only occasion where he prayed more than once. In the story of the widow's son, Elijah prayed three times before the child revived (1 Kings 17:17–22). We also find from studying his entire life that he was committed to a habit of prayer. He was consistent about communicating with the Lord.

Prayer consistency is probably the greatest ingredient to your prayers becoming prophetic "river" prayers. That is because you build upon the water. Instead of allowing a lapse of time to dry up your ground, you are flooding your ground with more and more spiritual water. This is how to turn your prayers from intimidated little trickles into loud, overflowing floodwaters. It begins with consistency to pray in both your natural language and in the Spirit. It is through the large quantity of watering in prayer that your life becomes flooded by the supernatural power of the Spirit.

This is a key to one of the most effective ways to enjoy the blessing of God in your life. Enjoying God's blessing means that you are successful in prayer. You get answers to what you pray. Look at Proverbs 8:34, which says, "Blessed is the man that heareth me, watching daily at my gates, waiting at the posts of my doors." This scripture lets us know that a daily commitment at the gates of the Lord is what causes you to hear Him. You become sensitive to the voice of the Spirit flowing through you. There is no question that consistency in prayer creates a flow in the river. It is wonderful to have a drink of water, but only one drink is not enough. An occasional drink will leave you thirsty, but consistent drinks of water will keep you lively and strong.

Rooms of Prayer

Now let me say it is not just consistency in prayer in general but rather consistency mixed with diversity in prayer. It is consistency in the many facets and expressions of prayer. Sometimes we get stuck in a rut or one flow of the Spirit. Train yourself to enter into different rooms in prayer on a regular basis. You need prayer both in the Spirit and in your understanding, as Paul said (1 Cor. 14:14–15). Then you also need prayer in intercession and spiritual warfare (Rom. 8:26). There is also worship in prayer and prayers of supplication or asking (John 14:14). Other kinds of prayer involve repentance and commitment to God (James 5:13–17; 1 John 1:9).

We need a well-rounded diet in our prayer life. Learn to explore the different "rooms" of prayer. There is something about using diversity in your prayer life that keeps you well balanced, strong, and anointed. It is comparable to a well-balanced diet where you get the full daily requirements of the right vitamins and minerals. If all you eat in your diet is broccoli, you will miss out on some important nutrition. Yes, broccoli is good for you, but you also need other valuable nutrients found in other foods. Don't get stuck in a rut in your prayers. Make yourself step into different things. Some prayers may be prayed loudly, while others may be quiet. Sometimes you may pray prostrate on the floor, while other times you may just sit on the couch or pace the room. Be diverse.

In the beginning, you may feel like you are just forcing the flow, but over time you will find yourself mightily navigating the rivers of the spirit in prayer that God wants to pull out of you. This practice will help you become sensitive to the anointing and better able to not only follow the moves of the Holy Spirit but also recognize the genuine things of God when you encounter them.

Boldness Unlocks the Rivers

For some reason, there seems to be something about a bold approach to prayer that unlocks the rivers of the Holy Spirit in you, whether it is prayer in the Spirit or prayer in your language of origin. It seems that the anointing is attracted to boldness. People who are bold, fearless, and confident in prayer seem to step into new places in the Spirit. They come away with a greater percentage of success in prayer than those who stay in a "safe," comfortable manner of prayer. Why is this true? Because I believe people who are bold in prayer tend to cultivate a faith environment, which is a key to answered prayer.

This key to prayer is what created such breakthrough success in the early church. Not only were the prayers of the early church bold, but also the disciples asked for boldness in their preaching. It takes raw boldness to enter new things in the Spirit. Timid people who always want to come across poised often won't grow into the supernatural and learn to cultivate it in their lives. That is not to say that because a person prays in a poised manner that it isn't effective. Instead, what we do have to explore are new expressions of boldness in prayer and know when and what environments are right for using them.

Look at this verse in Ephesians 3:12: "In Whom, because of our faith in Him, we dare to have boldness (courage and confidence) of free access (an unreserved approach to God with freedom and without fear)" (AMP). God wants us to approach Him with unreserved confidence—not a disrespectful attitude, but with strength and courage that are confident you have free access to God's throne (Heb. 4:16). That means you don't approach prayer with religious rhetoric. You approach it with the attitude that you came to accomplish something.

FOUR PRAYER RIVERS THAT FLOW OUT OF YOU

You can always recognize people who have learned to pray from the strength and rivers of their spirit. They have learned how to tap into the Holy Spirit inside of them. Their words are different and carry authority. The Pharisees noticed that Jesus's words carried power: "And they were astonished at his doctrine: for his word was with power" (Luke 4:32). They recognized there was something about Jesus's words that was different from everything else they had been hearing. His words had electricity about them. They were not the average sound.

This is the element you notice about people who pray from the river of the Holy Spirit flowing out of their belly. Their prayers carry power, and sometimes they even astonish people. When you step into prayer from the river of the Spirit, your sound will change.

We examined four ingredients needed for a well-balanced

and successful prayer life, but now we need to step into the different purposes or directions that our prayers are anointed for. What I mean is that when you and I pray, the Holy Spirit will have a direction or focus for us to follow. Sometimes that focus can apply to us or to someone else, but there will always be a direction the Spirit wants us pointed toward in our flow of prayer. We might better understand that form of prayer as an "unction." First John 2:20 says, "But ye have an unction from the Holy One, and ye know all things." This chapter in 1 John is talking about being anointed of the Holy Spirit so you can recognize truth from error. However, the focal point is that we have an unction or anointing from the Spirit to know which way He is leading us both in prayer and in daily living.

We have a tendency in our prayers, privately and corporately, to set the agenda rather than find the river of the Spirit for direction, meaning we don't always look to where the anointing is. Let's look here at the different directions or rivers of the Spirit we can enter into in prayer.

From the Book of Genesis, we can see a picture of four rivers that I believe prophetically represent the way the Holy Spirit anoints the direction and focus of our prayers. These four rivers are prophetic pictures of the anointing. In Genesis 2:10–14 we find that these four different rivers came out of Eden.

First, it is important to see that they came from Eden because Eden means "pleasure" and "delight." These rivers begin in the place of delight. Our place of delight is where God's Spirit lives in us. Adam and Eve once lived in a physical place of delight and pleasure. But through the infilling of the Holy Spirit, we are restored to that place of delight and pleasure—a spiritual Eden, so to speak.

Coming from Eden, these four rivers were divided into four heads, or four different directions. The Bible is showing us four main directions or categories that the Spirit in us wants our prayers to be focused upon. The Holy Spirit will anoint your prayers, regardless of the expression or methods, upon one or more of these rivers. It is important to find which river the Holy Spirit wants you flowing in and navigating at any given moment.

There were four of them because four is a biblical number that speaks of the earth's elements. We saw the elements— sun, moon, stars, and so on—created on the fourth day. We can also see that every room has four corners, just as the Bible says the earth has four corners and four directional winds (Rev. 7:1). Four also speaks of the earth's wind patterns that blow in four different directions. There are different ways in which the wind or anointing of the Holy Spirit will blow, which is why there were four rivers going different directions out of Eden. They speak of the Holy Spirit's anointing.

1. The river Pison

The meaning of this river is increase. Genesis 2:11–12 says, "The name of the first is Pison: that is it which compasseth the whole land of Havilah, where there is gold; and the gold of that land is good: there is bdellium and onyx stone." See how the river Pison surrounded the entire land of Havilah, which was a circular piece of land filled with gold. This river represents prosperity and provision. It is where we get our specific needs met in prayer.

From this we can see that the Spirit will anoint us in the river of provision. It is the flow of prayer where we petition for our needs and ask God for the things we desire. When we step into a river of asking, it is more than just requesting something from God, even though that is a part of it. When the anointing is there for it, you flow in this direction of prayer. Sometimes it may include actual financial provision, or it may involve other prayers and supplications to the Lord. There have been times where the Lord has anointed me in this kind of prayer and I just got supernaturally caught up praying scriptures, flipping through the pages of the Bible and praying them out one after another.

There was one occasion where a family came to me for prayer regarding an adoption/child custody situation they were involved with in court. They had many people praying, and I prayed with them also. However, it seemed that things just were not changing in court. The courts did not seem to be showing regard for certain legislation on the law books, and it seemed nothing was falling in their favor. This went on for several months, costing them a great deal in attorney's fees and court costs, which were impossible to pay for.

They periodically kept me up to date on the progress of the case through months of stressful days. Finally, I met with them one day when they were handed another blow from the court. I sat with them in a private room and this time became angry in the Spirit at the devil. Somehow, I stepped into the river Pison in prayer! We wrote a petition of prayer that stated we were now changing the legal directive of the natural court by overriding its decision with heaven's new court papers. We laid out scriptures and prayers on the sheet of paper.

We signed and dated it, and I literally took my fist and slammed it down on the table to represent the final decision of a judge's gavel coming down on the bench. We called upon the Great Judge of heaven, Almighty God. There was such an unction or river on how we prayed. God is my witness; within the week, and after months of fighting, their opponent completely dropped the case, giving them full custody. Not only that, but also their attorney canceled all the fees that had already accrued to several thousand dollars. There was an anointing that day to pray in a river or flow for provision. Praise the Lord!

Now I have prayed written petitions such as this one before, but never can I remember a time where we stepped into a river of it like this one. You could literally tell the Spirit of the Lord had put us in a river for provision and increase.

2. The river Gihon

Genesis 2:13 says, "And the name of the second river is Gihon: the same is it that compasseth the whole land of Ethiopia." The word *Gihon* means "a rushing stream bursting forth." It is the picture of water rushing through a flume and then bursting off the end of the slide like a waterfall. I like to think of it as the water in your garden hose. You can turn on the faucet, but you don't see the water immediately rushing through until all of a sudden it bursts forth out of the end of the hose. It is like a stream that moves along with a waterfall at the end of it that bursts forth and washes over things.

This river of prayer speaks of intercession and birthing in prayer. Some of the things we pray for are not going to be answered with a quick petition or request. They are going to be found as the waters of anointing in us rush along and then burst forth into the answer. It may not always be immediate as the answer is rushing and heading toward you. You may not readily see it, but it is on its way, until suddenly it bursts into manifestation. This river of prayer will involve your heart and often the expression of your entire internal being. The only other way to describe it is through the process of childbirth as the baby moves through the birthing canal and suddenly baby, water, and blood all burst forth, and then it's over. This kind of prayer from your spirit comes out of the depths of your being like that.

In 1 Samuel 1:9–13 Hannah gives us a glimpse into this river of prayer when she prayed to have a child. Her soul was poured forth out of her. It was almost as if she felt and gave birth to the child before she actually had Samuel. It was almost like living the reality of it, it was so real to her.

Jesus was another example of this river when He prayed in Gethsemane for the church that was about to be birthed (John 17). The Bible says during that particular time of prayer His sweat was like blood (Luke 22:44). He was in a flow of prayer that was with rushing intensity until there was a closure—a bursting forth.

Paul also prayed in this flow of prayer when he said, "I travail in birth again until Christ be formed in you" (Gal. 4:19). The familiar scripture in Romans 8:26 supports the river Gihon as a direction of prayer by the Spirit. It says, "Likewise the Spirit also helpeth our infirmities: for we know not what we should pray for as we ought: but the Spirit itself maketh intercession for us with groanings which cannot be uttered."

Often I have found that I can easily enter with the Holy Spirit into this flow of prayer when I just don't know how to pray about something. I just don't know where to begin. Every one of us have had those prayer times when we just need to pray in the Spirit so the Holy Spirit can pour out from us like that garden hose and pour His water over the person or situation.

Many people never get into the depths of this river of prayer, particularly in corporate settings, because this can be a long prayer river. It takes awhile to move downstream, and sometimes we don't have the patience for it. However, it is a flow where the Holy Spirit wants to take us and train us to navigate. I have prayed for many people and situations that wouldn't seem to turn around until I found the flow of the Holy Spirit in the river Gihon. In fact, by praying in the Spirit we can usually step into it.

Of course, there will be those times you will realize that there is not an unction or anointing there for this type of prayer, because for that situation this type of intercession isn't needed. You know when it is not "clicking." But then you are led into another direction in the Spirit, and you can sense the unction of the Holy Spirit on that.

This is why we need to stay sensitive and not just pray in the way we generally prefer. The Spirit may want to flow through you in a different direction, a different river flow.

3. The river Hiddekel

Genesis 2:14 reads: "And the name of the third river is Hiddekel: that is it which goeth toward the east of Assyria." I think this is one of the rivers the demons of hell hate the most in our prayer lives because it overwhelms them and takes away their territories. The word *Hiddekel* means "rapid water." This kind of water is white water. It is a rough, fast-moving current. It is a literal flash flood of prayer! We can begin to see the purpose of this river even more once we see the meaning surrounding Assyria, which is the exact location where this flooding river is heading. Assyria was the kingdom (also called Asshur) that was founded by Asshur and Nimrod. It was one of the kingdoms Nimrod built into his Babylonian empire that was the root of all demonism and paganism.

The word *Assyria* means "straightforward; successful." However, this is not speaking of the success that God gives us. It is success built on the spirit of humanism and pride, which is the essence of Lucifer. Nimrod was a type of Lucifer and his evil kingdom. Knowing this you can see why the Spirit of the Lord has a special prayer river pointed right toward Assyria! This river of rapid, forceful water is prayer that is about our authority in Christ and spiritual warfare. It is a flow of aggressive prayer against the forces of darkness.

This flow of prayer that comes from the Holy Spirit in us is like the water you see in films of the most dangerous forms of white-water rafting. It takes practice and spiritual skill. However, every believer filled with the Spirit has the weapons to pray from this river. The key is learning how to use those weapons accurately.

You don't want to step into the river Hiddekel just for fun. It is warfare prayer that has come to recover territories and nations from the power of darkness. While this prayer flow can operate very powerfully in your own prayer life, particularly when it comes to taking authority over the devil in your own situation, it works especially powerfully in corporate settings. God wants more churches to come together for prayer where they step into the river Hiddekel and pray in that flow for cities, nations, and territories—and not just now and then but regularly. Our world around us needs us to fight for them in this river of prayer. If we don't do it, who will? Our communities and governments could be left to the will of the devil.

Many Christians almost avoid this type of aggressive authority because it isn't the sweet happy kind of prayer many people enjoy. It is work. It takes strategizing with the Holy Spirit and the use of our spiritual weapons. In this kind of prayer we will use our spiritual weapons and address the spirits of darkness in the name of Jesus! This is the kind of prayer where you prophesy in the Spirit over regions and

decree the will of God to be established over them. You speak
into the atmosphere and declare the word of the Lord and call
upon the angels and the wonderful blood of Jesus. Often in
the river Hiddekel, it takes stepping into other tongues where
we allow the Holy Spirit to wage warfare that is beyond our
human wisdom and understanding.

We need to depend on that for the things we cannot
comprehend going on in the realm of the Spirit. We need
this river flow of the Spirit to come out of us to stop the force
of evil in our lives and areas of influence.

The important key to stepping into the flow of this river
is to do it when the Spirit is directing you into it. If the Lord
is not wanting you to go to war right then, then the flow of
prayer will not be upon Hiddekel. The mistake we make is
when we make this or another direction of prayer our only
focus. Again, we need all the rivers of prayer, not just the
ones that seem to go with the exciting trend of the day.

We have held prayer meetings where the flow of the Spirit
changed from river to river. Sometimes we began in one
anointing and ended in another. Other times we have actually been in a certain flow of the Spirit in prayer for a length
of time or season. The key is finding where the anointing is
flowing because the Holy Ghost knows what is needed, and
we need to follow Him there. If we get stuck too long in something and the Spirit of God has moved to another river, we
will be left praying with empty chatter and religious repeti-
tion. On the other hand, if you move off a particular anointing
too quickly, you may never complete the task God intended.
The key is to be flexible and open to the Holy Spirit.

Let me encourage you in something else. As you are
learning to follow the Holy Spirit as you pray from His
anointing in you, there will be times for "practice." Hiddekel

prayers can be some of the most challenging to become skillful in, especially in a corporate setting. When God first began to use our church this way in spiritual warfare, there were some meetings that were choppy and felt like everyone was drowning in that river. I like to picture a guy who is learning to kayak. Most of the time in the beginning, he is upside down!

We had some prayer meetings like that. We knew what the Holy Spirit wanted, but we were still in the beginning stages of knowing how to follow His lead in prayer. We had a few visitors during those times whom we never saw again, but God knew our hearts were trying to step into a new river. And to our credit there were newcomers who saw God's purpose and stayed. Now we have learned as a church how to navigate some of those rapids. When the Holy Spirit is directing us into that river we can follow Him right in there.

Give yourself, your church, and your prayer group some grace. No matter what river of prayer you step into, it takes practice and persistence to learn how to flow there. You have to learn how to navigate the waters in the spirit of prayer. If you will not be afraid of new sounds and different expressions, you will learn to pray from the river of your spirit, where it is no longer forced religious prayers but prayer that you ride until it produces miracles.

4. The river Euphrates

Genesis 2:14 tells us that "the fourth river is Euphrates." I am certain that it is no coincidence that the Bible lists these four rivers in the order it does. If we look, we can see a progression. We begin with asking God (Pison River), to birthing and intercession (Gihon River), then on to spiritual warfare (Hiddekel River), and then we come to the center of it all—the river Euphrates. The word *Euphrates* means "fruitfulness." Notice that it is the fourth and final direction of prayer. Not only is that because a fruitful life is the result of anointed prayer, but also I believe it is in line with the fourth day, the Day of Pentecost, which we talked about in previous chapters. This is the fourth river of prayer that comes from the Spirit of the Lord inside you. It is the essence and powerful result of Pentecost, the Holy Ghost within. It is the river that produces the fruit of the Spirit.

The river Euphrates will accomplish a twofold purpose in your life: fruit for personal growth and fruit for ministry.

The first purpose in this river of prayer is for you to grow and consecrate yourself as a Christian. It can involve commitment and repentance. When we pray from this river, we bear fruit as believers because we mature and become like Christ. The second purpose of this river of prayer is for the purpose of your call to ministry and action in the kingdom. Prayers in the flow of the river Euphrates paved the way for miracles, signs, and wonders in the ministry of the apostles and the early church. The Book of Acts records repeatedly how they went from house to house and made a lifestyle of prayer (Acts 2:42, 46). This particular flow of prayer is what makes you and stabilizes your entire Christian life. It is the essence and foundation of your relationship with God. Without regular prayers of communion, fellowship, and intimacy with the Lord, you will find yourself unproductive, unfruitful, and not growing as a Christian. The river Euphrates is the mightiest, most important flow of prayer that we need to develop in our lives.

Notice that when the angel poured the vial on the river Euphrates in Revelation 16:12, it was dried up. Once this river ran dry, it released and made a way for demons and unclean spirits to operate. This very important river creates purity and fruit. Without it, we leave our ground a haven for evil spirits. Of all the rivers mentioned in Genesis 2:10–14, this river is the one the Bible often calls the great river (Josh. 1:4; Rev. 9:14; 16:12). This great river in prayer will swallow up evil in our lives and produce the miraculous.

Look at Jeremiah 51:61–64, which gives us an amazing prophetic picture of the river Euphrates.

> And Jeremiah said to Seraiah, When thou comest to Babylon, and shalt see, and shalt read all these words; then shalt thou say, O Lord, thou hast spoken against this place, to cut it off, that none shall remain in it, neither man nor beast, but that it shall be desolate for ever. And it shall be, when thou hast made an end of reading this book, that thou shalt bind a stone to it, and cast it into the midst of Euphrates: And thou shalt say, Thus shall Babylon sink, and shall not rise from the evil that I will bring upon her: and they shall be weary.

Of course these verses have a literal and historical significance on the earth, but as a prophetic example of prayer it shows us that all worldly influence in our lives is swallowed up by the power of the Euphrates. The darkness that tries to keep us bound is destroyed in this river of prayer, leaving only a fruitful life filled with the anointing and power of God.

Worship is part of the prayer that flows from the river Euphrates. We can see how Paul and Silas worshiped God in the prison cell (Acts 16), and their flow of prayer caused the fruit of miracles, signs, and wonders. The only way to learn to flow in this river of the Holy Spirit is by spending time alone with the Spirit of God. Enoch seemed to be a man who flowed in this river of the Spirit. He walked with God so much that he didn't die; God took him, and he just left (Gen. 5:24)! By a deep, close, and personal prayer relationship with God you learn to pray from the great flow of the river Euphrates.

A wonderful example of this is when I heard a preacher ask one time, "If someone asked you to stand up and talk to God about all His attributes one right after another, without having to think about it, how long could you stand there and do it? Would you only be able to list five or ten things and then begin to stumble at what to say?" When we have a life where we flow from our spirit in prayer with God, we will never run out of things to say. You begin to run away with God, just you and Him. This flow in the Spirit is where the secrets of God are flowing; it is where the miracles are and the supernatural manifests, just as it did for Enoch.

Psalm 42:7–8 says, "Deep calleth unto deep at the noise of thy waterspouts: all thy waves and thy billows are gone over me. Yet the LORD will command his lovingkindness in the daytime, and in the night his song shall be with me, and my prayer unto the God of my life." The river Euphrates is a deep river. It is the place where we step into the depths of God that are only found by a deep relationship. You can learn to step into it by worship, praying, and singing in the Spirit and by just talking and spending time with the Father. In this flow of prayer you also listen to His voice. Notice in verse 8 above that the noise of God's waterfalls is heard in the call of the deep.

This flow of prayer should be private, and it is also found in our corporate time of worship and prayer of just waiting and listening in the presence of the Lord. It is not religious and quiet only. Waterfalls and deep water have a unique sound, but this river of prayer carries the anointing of the weighty things of God. It is the heavy glory of His Spirit resting upon you and resting upon a people. Make a life habit of flowing in prayer in the river Euphrates, for that is where the supernatural things of God are!

FUNCTION FROM THE UNCTION

"Function from the unction." Have you ever heard that phrase used in a church setting before? I have. We have all sorts of clichés in the church, and this one is no exception. However, it is nonetheless a true one. The best place to find the supernatural at work is to locate when and where the unction or anointing is moving. We cannot be afraid to function by following the different unctions of the Holy Spirit as He leads you into them. When you feel the anointing moving in one direction or another, then begin to allow the move of the Spirit to carry you into it without always worrying about what it sounds like or what others might think.

First John 2:27–28 says, "But the anointing which ye have received of him abideth in you, and ye need not that any man teach you: but as the same anointing teacheth you of all things, and is truth, and is no lie, and even as it hath taught you, ye shall abide in him. And now, little children, abide in him; that, when he shall appear, we may have confidence, and not be ashamed before him at his coming." We can be confident that the anointing in us will pull us in one direction or another, and we have to trust it. Be careful not to allow all your previous religious and learned habits to keep you from experiencing new and fresh things in God when you pray. God is a big God, and He has much contained in His Spirit inside of you. He wants you and me to learn how to flow with Him and pray in a new level of anointing. It is in the flow of prayer that supernatural results and miracles will be produced.

Chapter Eight

UNLEASHING YOUR
FLOODWATERS OF BLESSING

W E HAVE TALKED all through this book about how
the Bible points to a very powerful river of the
Holy Spirit that is inside of us, a river that carries
supernatural ability. I want to draw your attention back to
the verse where it all began with what Jesus said about you.
Look at John 7:38–39 again; it says, "He that believeth on me,
as the scripture hath said, out of his belly shall flow rivers of
living water. (But this spake he of the Spirit, which they that
believe on him should receive: for the Holy Ghost was not yet
given; because that Jesus was not yet glorified.)"

Let's briefly recap what we have covered in the pages of
this book and then talk about how to keep God's supernatural floodwaters of blessing flowing over your life every day.

First, we learned that when the Holy Spirit was given on
the Day of Pentecost, He made His mighty power available
to live in your very own spirit. His miracles were deposited
in you. His power, grace, healing, prosperity, and peace were
all downloaded into your spirit. By pouring Himself into
you, He poured into you rivers of living water. This moment
in history changed us forever from being empty into being
full of supernatural power. In that regard, Pentecost was a
pivotal event that changed history. It changed the disciples

from weak, insecure people into those who turned their world upside down. They made a mark on the world because they unleashed the floodwaters of the Spirit over their cities and regions. This deposit in them came in the form of something known as a river. Ezekiel prophesied about it. Moses only wished he could have experienced it. Although he didn't understand what it was, he knew something on the inside with missing. He only got to see God's glory on the outside, but when he left the mountain, he walked away empty.

On the other hand, you and I are baptized in the Holy Ghost. The power of the living God Himself rushed to live within us and is an ever-available source of supernatural supply. The river of God in you is a well of living water that is powerful enough to deliver and to heal and set you free. Inside of you is a powerful supply that you can depend on and draw from to help you deal with the situations you face in life every day. That anointing will change circumstances with the flood of living water because the Spirit of the Lord has given you an eternal spiritual supply. You can be assured that God did not leave you destitute of any good thing He has available. After all, you are the house of the Holy Spirit—His dwelling place—and He has seen to it that His home is well equipped, furnished, and supplied so that He can display Himself with might and power through your life!

Once you learn to tap into the river of God coming from within you, you can be sure that you will experience many mighty miracles and blessings. Yes, the enemy may try many things to keep you from believing that you have been mightily anointed this way. He will work overtime to try to get you into fear so that you do not trust what you carry or believe you are able to walk in the power of God you have received. Just remind the devil and yourself that you are anointed. In fact, speak to yourself and say, "I am anointed!" Don't jump out of the river; determine to stay in there and use what God has given you. There are many places you can go and enjoy in the Holy Ghost once you determine that you will live from the well of your spirit. You can see yourself manifest miracles, healing, and peace. The gifts of the Spirit will work in your life. You can take prayer to whole new levels and learn to pray from the rivers of the Spirit in you. In the well of your spirit are the depths of God, because that is where His Spirit resides. You can draw from that supply in prayer so that your prayer life reaches a place where it begins to flow freely and is something you love. The power of God will work in your life when you live from what the Holy Spirit brought you in the well of your spirit.

I trust that after reading this book your life in the Spirit will reach new heights, and perhaps for the first time you will see yourself as the anointed vessel of the Holy Ghost that you are! You may just want to repeat that one more time. Say, "I am anointed!"

Here I want to give you some practical ways to live from the well of your spirit. They will help keep your spiritual river at the flood stage so it can wash powerfully over the obstacles of life. I would encourage you to read them and meditate on them so that when you feel like you are powerless because of a trial, you will be reminded that your well of supply is waiting for you to take another drink and let the river flow. It will cause you to unleash the floodwaters of God that will carry you into a life of supernatural blessings.

1. Believe that you are full of power!

In Acts 3:4, Peter said, "Look on us." He knew the anointing he had received and carried inside him. Talk about what you received and, like Peter, say, "Look on me." Talk to yourself on a regular basis about the anointing you have received from God. Read about it in the Bible and commit scriptures like John 7:37–39 to memory. Get the fact that you are anointed in power down into your heart. Eliminate from your life words of rejection and failure. They will only tell you that you are powerless, which is an absolute lie. Believe you are anointed today. If you only have a halfhearted revelation of it, you won't live in it. Remember, say these words every day: "I am anointed!"

2. Draw from your river.

In Acts 3:6, Peter said, "In the name of Jesus Christ of Nazareth rise up and walk." To learn to use your well of anointing, you have to draw from it and use it regularly in situations the way Peter did. You draw through your words and by your actions. When Peter did that, the man at the gate was healed. Make declarations aloud, and speak about the miracle you want produced. You don't have to begin by raising a lame man, but you should most certainly start in your own life. For example, start drawing from your river by speaking to that pain in your body and commanding it to leave.

3. Pray in the Spirit.

Jude 20 says, "But ye, beloved, building up yourselves on your most holy faith, praying in the Holy Ghost." Praying in tongues is probably the most powerful way to fill your well to overflowing. It builds you up like nothing else because it carries power that does the work for you. The more I pray in the Spirit, the less I have to push myself. The Spirit carries me, and I just go along for the ride. It is so much easier that way. It unlocks the Holy Spirit from within you and brings you into the supernatural.

4. Cultivate boldness and zeal.

Second Timothy 1:6–7 says, "Wherefore I put thee in remembrance that thou stir up the gift of God, which is in thee by the putting on of my hands. For God hath not given us the spirit of fear; but of power, and of love, and of a sound mind." If you are the shy, quiet type, then learn to break out of that. There is something about a bold, zealous approach that breaks religious bondage and overtakes fear. The anointing is attracted to it. Stir yourself up in power; it's OK. It is like the football team that gets psyched up before a game. Dance, rejoice, praise, and shout. When you stir yourself with zeal, the water will begin to flow. If you feel better to start out by yourself, then put on an anointed praise CD and dance to it before the Lord. When you go to church and people begin to praise God all over the place, then make sure you aren't the one holding back. Be bold and step into it.

5. Stay in the river!

Psalm 1 shows us that when we are planted by rivers of water, we will bear fruit. Sometimes it will seem more profitable to uproot ourselves and jump out, then come up with something else for the answer. Even though there may be times it will feel like nothing is working and nothing is changing, just stay in the way of the Spirit. Don't get frustrated and give up. Remember, some situations won't crumble until after the waves have beat on them for a long time, so just stay in the water of the Holy Spirit. Sometimes it takes time to learn how to flow from that well, but with practice you will do it powerfully.

6. Continually refill the well.

Ephesians 5:18–20 gives us the secrets to refilling the well of the Spirit in us. It says, "And be not drunk with wine,

217

wherein is excess; but be filled with the Spirit; speaking to yourselves in psalms and hymns and spiritual songs, singing and making melody in your heart to the Lord; giving thanks always for all things unto God and the Father in the name of our Lord Jesus Christ." You can continually refill your well of power by speaking to yourself, worshiping God, and voicing your heart of thanks to the Lord. We can spend so much time filling ourselves with natural things until our lives have become "drunk" with them instead. Paul's letter to the Ephesians teaches us to immerse ourselves around things that pertain to the Spirit so our well will be full. Prayer is a part of that. Reading your Bible and studying Scripture is also part of it. The more time you spend in spiritual things, the more full your well will become.

7. Connect your well with the body of Christ.

Isaiah 2:3 says, "Come, let us go up to the mountain of the LORD, to the house of the God of Jacob" (NIV). The verses of Isaiah chapter 2 show a corporate setting of God's people. No matter what anyone ever told you or said to the contrary, you need to be around other on-fire believers who can keep you in the flow. You need a pastor and church family for your river to have a purpose and to also receive strength. In the Book of Acts, the early church met both in homes and at the temple (Acts 2:46) because they recognized the strength of numbers. You may not always agree with people, the church, or your pastor, but you need them nevertheless. They will keep your river flowing strong. Even in the ministry, I cannot tell you how many times I have been exhausted before heading over to midweek prayer service, but after we gather together in the Spirit I am always so refreshed and filled up again. It empowers you through the week. There is special anointing reserved for the corporate atmosphere.

Your Floodwaters of Blessing

When the prophet Ezekiel saw this incredible vision (Ezek. 47:1–12) of the river of God flooding out of the house of God (you and I), it was an overflowing river that could not be crossed. He saw a foreshadowing of the event of Pentecost. We talked toward the beginning of this book about the source of the river he saw, but now here at the end we will see the result of the floodwaters. When these waters start to flow freely in our lives, they will do some very powerful things, which are all meant for our deliverance, our enjoyment, and our blessing. Are you ready to see them? Stir your faith right now because every last one of those things belongs to you.

Before we cover these floodwaters for the remainder of the book, I want to remind you of the power of water. I remember several years ago when the tidal wave hit Indonesia. The results were devastating. Nothing that the water covered was spared. Thousands perished, and the destruction was beyond comparison. From that one event we can see that water is a powerful force. It is no wonder that the Lord compared His power to a mighty river of water. The difference is that He is the fountain of *living* water (Jer. 2:13), which has come to give life. When the water of the Holy Spirit washes over things, nothing will remain the same. Everything is affected. This is what Ezekiel saw take place, and this is what will happen to us when the floodwaters of God begin to take over.

Everything Must Live

The message God was trying to get across here is amazing. Look at Ezekiel 47:9, which says, "And it shall come to pass, that every thing that liveth, which moveth, whithersoever the rivers shall come, *shall live*" (emphasis added). From this you can receive faith that anytime the devil tries to lie and tell you that you are going to die prematurely, you can look him square in the eye and say no! When the rivers of your spirit wash over a situation, over your life, over your body, *they are going to live!* Where do you need life today? There is life inside the well of your spirit. Speak life to yourself, your situation, and on behalf of those you love.

I once heard a story about a man of God who was in a room of people who were all talking about the dangers of plane crashes. He stood up and said, "No plane will crash while I am on it!" He had a revelation that he carried life and power. On another occasion, a preacher was sitting in a room of other ministers who were all talking about their medicines, herbal remedies, and other aches and ailments. When they asked this minister what his secret was, he simply replied, "First Peter 2:24 still works for me!" With that, everyone in the room changed the subject. Of course, 1 Peter 2:24 says, "...by whose stripes ye were healed." He too had a revelation that Jesus gave him abundant life right here on this earth.

When you have the rivers of the Holy Spirit flowing from your life, you can expect to live. Believe that the waters have come and caused you to live right now.

THE MULTITUDE OF FISH—THE MAGNIFICENT SUPPLY

Ezekiel also saw fish in this river. They speak of financial blessing and provision. Ezekiel 47:9 says, "And there shall be a very great multitude of fish, because these waters shall come thither." The reason the multitude of fish always speaks of increase is because Jesus multiplied fish to show Himself as the God of provision when He fed the multitude (Matt. 14:19; Mark 6:41; Luke 9:16). He also took a coin from the mouth of a fish to pay taxes (Matt. 17:27), and He filled the fishing nets of the disciples (Luke 5:6).

These were all examples of supernatural provision from the Spirit of God. That is why when Ezekiel saw that water produce an abundance of fish, he was seeing God reveal a picture of prosperity. Jesus said that He came to give us life abundantly (John 10:10). Well, by giving you His Spirit to dwell with you, there is a fountain of provision just waiting to wash over your financial situation today. It is there to help you turn things around. You don't have to try to believe that spiritual water is going to help you win the sweepstakes. You just need to get it flowing over your current job situation and bring stability to that. Expect every day that you will wake up to a "multitude of fish" or provision that is there for you to enjoy. Don't begin by trying to look for millions of dollars in your river; some people just need to use their fishing net to find their next meal. However, the more you do that and begin to learn the "art of fishing" and look for your blessing in the river of provision the Spirit has put in you, you will begin to grow and be filled until eventually the blessing and provision of God will flood you on every side. You can count on it. There is multitude of fish, which is quite a magnificent supply of provision.

LET HEALING WATERS WASH OVER ME

Then Ezekiel saw more in this river of living water. Not only did he see life produced and a multitude of fish, but he also saw healing. Ezekiel 47:9 also says, "...for they shall be healed; and every thing shall live whither the river cometh." God is so wanting us to see that He is committed to giving us powerful life that He repeats it again, but this time He mentions another word, *healing*. Now people will say any number of things about healing. Some are for bodily healing, while others are determined that the Bible only promises internal, spiritual healing. However, I think all of the above are correct, because no scripture really specifies.

In fact, I heard a story one time about a man who had some serious physical heart problems and who stood on the promise in Psalm 57:7, which says, "My heart is fixed, O God, my heart is fixed: I will sing and give praise." Now most translations of this verse will state that it means that my heart is steadfast on the Lord. However, he believed God wanted him healed and that his literal heart was going to be repaired by the power of God. Do you know what happened? That's right; he got healed. He didn't get hung up religiously; he just knew that the Bible is a healing book and he needed to be healed.

Healing is healing; if it hurts and needs to be healed, then the river of the Spirit can wash over it and heal it. If your body hurts, then physical healing is important to you. Trust in the promise of healing for your body then. If your emotional heart is broken, then healing also belongs to you as well. Allow the Word of healing to put salve upon the pain. The river of healing lives on the inside of you because of the Holy Ghost.

In John 5, we find the story of the pool of Bethesda. For thirty-eight years, an angel would stir the waters of this special pool. Then, while the waters were still in motion, the first person who could make it into the water would be healed. The Bible says there were crowds of people there. That is because people everywhere want to be well.

Nothing has changed today; people don't want to hurt and suffer, so why would God stop the healing flow? Just like then, He wants people to be well. God wants you well today! The problem with the pool of Bethesda was that you could only be healed if you could touch the healing water. Well, there was a lame man there who could never seem to make it into the water, but one day Jesus came by. Oh, what a day for this man! Jesus asked the man one simple question. He said, "Sir, do you want to be well?" What do you suppose any person in his condition would have said? "Yes, I want to be well!" Jesus didn't have to carry the man into the healing waters because He came that day to show us that He is the healing water and He has given us His Spirit. The pool of healing water is living in you—river of living water. Don't put pressure on yourself for the healing; just smile today as you lean back in your chair and rest in that river. Today, you can rest and say, "Come, healing waters. Wash over me."

And Souls Will Come to My River

Not only do you have to rejoice at the life, blessing, and healing that God has placed in the river of your spirit, but you also can be excited that this anointing will draw hungry, hurting, and lost people to you. That can include friends and relatives you have been praying for, and they will come to the Lord.

Look at Ezekiel 47:10, which says, "And it shall come to pass, that the fishers shall stand upon it [the river] from En-gedi even unto En-eglaim; they shall be a place to spread forth nets; their fish shall be according to their kinds, as the fish of the great sea, exceeding many."

Now let's see the prophetic revelation in this verse. In the previous verses of Ezekiel 47, we saw how the fish reference was in relation to prosperity. But in verse 10, it is a little different. The reason it is different is because this is the first time fisherman are mentioned. It says that they shall stand upon the river between two locations. The first is En-gedi, which means "the fountain of a kid (goat)," and the other is En-eglaim, which is "the fountain of two calves." That means this river of living waters runs between the place of goats and the place of two calves.

Goats always speak of the lost. The two calves provide a picture of the pairs of oxen that carried the molten sea (2 Chron. 4:1–4). The molten sea is a picture of many rivers flowing together as the church—one large body of water—and its message is carried by God's anointed vessels, which are you and me. This is further depicted in those whom Jesus sent into the world in pairs to preach the gospel two by two as the representatives of the presence of God (Mark 6:7–13).

This river of living water is the connecting force between the lost and those who have come to present the gospel. Ezekiel 47:10 says that fishers will stand upon this anointing or river of the Spirit. The result will be that they will spread their nets and take in many fish. Jesus said in Matthew 4:19, "Follow me, and I will make you fishers of men." The river of anointing in you will make you successful in winning the lost. If you will exercise your faith that you are anointed to win the lost, then the Holy Spirit will cause your river to minister and win many fish for Christ. There is an anointing in the river of the Spirit to touch the world just as the early church turned their world upside down and won thousands into the kingdom.

The Tree Is Growing Tall

Now if all of that was not enough, the vision of Ezekiel tells much more of what God has put in this wonderful river of anointing. Ezekiel 47:12 says, "On this side and on that side, shall grow all trees for meat, whose leaf shall not fade, neither shall the fruit thereof be consumed: it shall bring forth new fruit according to his months." The Bible refers to trees like you and me who are planted by rivers of water (Ps. 1:3). We are planted in the river of the Holy Spirit where we are watered and grow in spiritual things. Here we grow so that we are good for mature meat or mature revelation. Then our leaves will not fade, which shows that mature trees are not moved by drought and storms. Our fruit is not subject to the effects of an attack, and regardless of the conditions, we will keep bearing fresh new fruit in our lives. The richness and success that the well of the Holy Spirit in us provides are almost indescribable. They paint a picture of people whose lives are drenched in the total greatness and wonder of God Himself. I am so glad the fullness of the Holy Spirit is in me, aren't you?

BECAUSE THE WATERS ISSUED OUT

Of course, Ezekiel 47:11 continues to say that all these blessings are because of this powerful anointing the Holy Spirit brought when He filled you. It is all "because their waters they issued out of the sanctuary: and the fruit thereof shall be for meat, and the leaf thereof for medicine." Our lives, and those in the world around us, get to experience the might and blessing of God Himself because His Spirit and the living water He gives is flooding out of us. We don't have to walk through life destitute, just hoping we will find a touch somewhere. We have fruit that will sustain us, and in our leaves is healing medicine. From the very depths of our being the waters of life flow. We can look to the Spirit of God Himself who will make us stable, successful examples of His power. All we have to do is set ourselves to believe it.

I want to give you a few final practical pointers to help

solidify this revelation inside your heart. You may be saying right now, "I understand what you are saying, but you just don't realize that I have tried everything. I don't think this will change my situation." We can always hide behind the fact that someone does not understand the trouble we are facing or the pain we have experienced.

Maybe you want to step into what the Holy Spirit has given you, but past experience has made you think it is too good to be true. Not one of us can perfectly understand the feelings behind another person's personal experiences. What we can understand equally and universally are the promises and power of God. The only way to get past the reality of what we have been through is by the supernatural power of the Holy Spirit and our willingness to believe it. Start walking in the supernatural by believing it.

The Bible says in Ephesians 5:26, "That he might sanctify and cleanse it with the washing of water by the word." This is speaking about us, the church. The Spirit of the Lord can cleanse you from all previous experiences and current frustrations by washing you again with the water of His Word. Let His river overflow you today without the reservation that it might work for someone else but not for you. It will work for you!

MOAB IS MY WASHBASIN

Let any reservation that you are anything less than the dynamite power of God be put aside. Every trial that seems to be too big for the anointing of God today is under your feet. That is more than just an encouraging saying.

Psalm 60:8 gives us one more powerful glimpse about the river of the Holy Spirit that will place every trial under your feet. It says, "Moab is my washbasin" (NIV). Moab, of course, represents a type of the world filled with all of the filth of life. David said in this psalm that Moab was to become his washbasin, which was a place to wash the feet. These words speak to how water washes over your feet when they are soiled from travel and how you can be assured that this world and the pain it brings will only serve to be the washbasin to catch what the river of God's supernatural power has washed out of your life. Your enemies and the trials of this life are washed under your feet by the fountain of living water today. Luke 10:19 says that you carry the power to walk over all the power of the devil. Rather than allow the world to run over you, decide that it is nothing more than a place to wash your feet while the river of anointing floods your life.

You were designed as a Spirit-filled believer not to live a life of desperation but to live powerfully from the well of your spirit. It doesn't have to be a challenge, but it does have to be a lifestyle. The early church stepped into it once they experienced the impartation of Pentecost, and every day they produced the miraculous wherever they went. You have received the power of God, the gifts of the Holy Spirit, and His might. There is nothing that you cannot accomplish in God's promised blessing when you live your life powerfully from the well of your own spirit and discover how to become the supernatural you!

To activate and receive what you have read in these pages, pray this prayer with me:

> *Father, I thank You that I can rise up in the power*
> *of the Holy Spirit in me today. I am supernatural!*
> *I draw from the well of the Spirit in me, the foun-*
> *tain of living water. I declare that this water will*
> *wash over and flood every situation in my life right*
> *now. I call upon the anointing of the Spirit to wash*

*over*_____ [name your situations or persons for whom you are praying], *and I say that this situation aligns itself with the Word and promises of God. I call miracles out of my spirit. I call the supernatural out of my spirit. I say that I am anointed to do great signs and wonders and that the gifts of the Holy Spirit will operate through me with precision and accuracy. As the river of anointing washes through me today, I receive all the healing, provision, increase, and grace to accomplish the will of God for my life. I have come to flood my life and the world around me with the power of the living God. I am anointed today, and I draw upon the well in me, the well of the Holy Spirit! In Jesus's name, amen!*

ONE VOICE MINISTRIES
The Ministry of Hank & Brenda Kunneman

Conferences

Hank and Brenda travel worldwide, ministering in churches, conferences, and conventions. They bring relevant biblical messages from a prophetic viewpoint, and their dynamic preaching style is coupled with the demonstrations of the Holy Spirit. Though they preach at events separately, they are especially known for their unique platform of ministry together as a team in the ministry of the gifts of the Spirit. For additional information about scheduling a ministry or church conference with Hank and/or Brenda, you may contact One Voice Ministries at 402.896.6692, or you may request a ministry packet online at www.ovm.org

Books, Products, and Resources

Books, audio, and video materials are available at the Kunnemans' online store at www.ovm. org. Book titles include *The Supernatural You*, *The Revealer of Secrets*, *When Your Life Has Been Tampered With*, *Hide and Seek*, *Don't Leave God Alone*, and *Chaos in the King's Court*. The One Voice Ministries' Web site also provides many ministry resources, including Hank's page called "Prophetic Perspectives" that provides excerpts and prophetic insight on world events. Brenda's page, "The Daily Prophecy," has changed lives around the world. There are also numerous articles for study.

Lord of Hosts Church

Hank and Brenda Kunneman also pastor Lord of Hosts Church in Omaha, Nebraska. Filled with captivating praise and worship and sound, prophetic teaching, services at Lord of Hosts Church are always rich with the presence of God. Lord of Hosts Church is known for its solid team

of leaders, organized style and ministry that touches the everyday needs of people. Through the many avenues of ministry the church is raising up strong believers. Many ministries worldwide have referred to Lord of Hosts Church to be among the most up-and-coming, cutting-edge churches in the United States. For further information about Lord of Hosts Church, call 402.896.6692 or visit online at www.lohchurch.org or www.ovm.org.

PASTORS HANK AND BRENDA KUNNEMAN
LORD OF HOSTS CHURCH AND ONE VOICE MINISTRIES

5351 S. 139th Plaza
Omaha, Nebraska 68137

Phone: (402) 896-6692
Fax: (402) 894-9068

www.ovm.org
www.lohchurch.org

FREE NEWSLETTERS
TO HELP EMPOWER YOUR LIFE

Why subscribe today?

☐ **DELIVERED DIRECTLY TO YOU.** All you have to do is open your inbox and read.

☐ **EXCLUSIVE CONTENT.** We cover the news overlooked by the mainstream press.

☐ **STAY CURRENT.** Find the latest court rulings, revivals, and cultural trends.

☐ **UPDATE OTHERS.** Easy to forward to friends and family with the click of your mouse.

CHOOSE THE E-NEWSLETTER THAT INTERESTS YOU MOST:

- Christian news
- Daily devotionals
- Spiritual empowerment
- And much, much more

SIGN UP AT: **http://freenewsletters.charismamag.com**

8178